Lots of Love to

dear Uncle Jimmy

the 3 L's.

Playing for Rangers No. 4

PLAYING FOR RANGERS
No. 4

Edited by KEN GALLACHER

STANLEY PAUL/LONDON

STANLEY PAUL & CO LTD
3 Fitzroy Square, London W1

AN IMPRINT OF THE HUTCHINSON GROUP

London Melbourne Sydney Auckland
Wellington Johannesburg Cape Town
and agencies throughout the world

First published 1972

*This book has been set in Linotron Baskerville, printed in Great Britain
by offset litho by Flarepath Printers Ltd., St. Albans, Herts.
and bound by William Brendon of Tiptree, Essex*

ISBN 0 09 112660 6

Contents

Barcelona brings success and a Change at the top

Rangers had been in Europe for sixteen long years before they eventually won the Continental cup the Ibrox fans had dreamed of through the seasons of failure. . . .

And it was appropriate that the trophy which now stands in the glittering trophy room of Ibrox should have been the European Cup Winners Cup. For Rangers were one of the clubs who pioneered the tournament for national Cup winners when it began in 1960 with just ten clubs entering for that initial competition! Now the tournament has grown to rival the European Champions' Cup . . . and is far more important than the European Union, or one-time Fairs Cup.

In that first season Rangers reached the final for the first time, defeating formidable opposition on the way. In the first round they beat Ferencvaros of Hungary, then Borussia Munchen Gladbach were disposed of and in the semi-final Wolves were knocked out by the Scots. But in a two-legged final—it was played on a home-and-away basis at that time, Rangers went down on a 3–1 aggregate score to a star-studded Italian team, Fiorentina.

Then, in 1967, Rangers had reached the final of the Cup Winners' Cup competition for the second time only to lose in extra time to Bayern Munich in a Nuremberg final which had been virtually a home match for the West Germans.

Eventually, in Barcelona, the Rangers gained the reward they had searched for in those long and sometimes bitter years of disappointment in Europe. Immediately the players had become in Manager Willie Waddell's own words—Ibrox Immortals' . . . because they had done what no other Rangers' team had ever been able to do. They had taken a European trophy back to Ibrox!

The scenes when the trophy was brought back to Glasgow will never be forgotten by the players or by the twenty five thousand fans who were at Ibrox on a night of teeming rain to get a glimpse of the trophy that meant so much to all of them. Many more thousands of supporters were still journeying back from Spain but those who were at Ibrox cheered the players as they went round the track in an open lorry.

Pipe bands played, the fans sang and danced and wept with joy on the terracings and the players in their royal blue track suits brandished the Cup that had become a symbol of greatness for every one of them. It was a night of magic and no one among the fans or the players realised that just two weeks later there were to be dramatic changes in the Ibrox management structure.

The shock came exactly two weeks after the Barcelona triumph at a press conference which Manager Willie Waddell had called in the plush surroundings of the Blue Room at Ibrox. The assembled pressmen were in the room when Waddell entered along with coach Jock Wallace. And these were the two men most closely affected by the blunt announcement which was made without preamble.

Waddell, architect of Rangers' triumph in Barcelona and Wallace, his right hand man were scarcely seated when Waddell announced—'From now on Jock Wallace will be known as team manager of Rangers and he will be totally responsible for all matters concerning the team and players, including team selections.'

Then Waddell, boss at Ibrox for two and a half years, added: 'I become general manager of the club and more or less still in the number one position. There is no significance in this move beyond the need to streamline our set-up. I have never made any secret of the fact that team management is a young man's game in my opinion and it becomes more and more difficult these days for one man to run the entire show. There is a great deal of work involved in the running of a big club, especially when there is the European scene to consider as well as the home front.

'I have always felt that the time to make changes is when you have success . . . rather than wait until changes are forced upon you. Jock Wallace played a big part in our European success and I have every confidence that he will take over the playing side now and handle it with distinction.

'Over the two years we have been together Jock and I have established a good working relationship and that will continue. Jock has, of course, gained the respect of the players in his time as coach and this will benefit him enormously now

Jock Wallace, on left, and Willie Waddell, the two men who
guide Rangers towards greatness. . . .

that he has sole control. I have no fears for the team's future with Jock in charge.'

The fifty-year-old Waddell—that birthday celebrated with a champagne party in Italy on the eve of the game against Torino—insisted—'Jock is in complete charge of training, tactics and team selection and though we will be working closely I know that he will never be a puppet on a string. He is his own man and I respect him for that.'

Wallace, blunt, straight talking, a rough diamond and a self-admitted hard task-master as far as players are concerned, had realised an ambition. He had always wanted to become manager of a top club in his own right . . . always wanted to be the man who had to make the decisions and mould the team. The chance had been given to him and he knew the challenges he had to face when he accepted.

He said simply—'I know that the main change for me is going to be that the decisions have to be made alone. And I am the man who has to make them. In the past I have given advice on various aspects but the final decision on the team matters has rested with the Boss.

'Obviously the main challenge that faces me now is to try to beat Celtic in the First Division championship. Well, they did better than us last year at home . . . but we did better than they did in Europe and that shouldn't be forgotten. But I have to try to get success at home. I have my own ideas and because of that I'm not going to be too worried about what Jock Stein does or how Jock Stein works.

Willie Waddell, now general manager, in the dug-out role he will now hand over to Jock Wallace.

'I will stick to my own ideas and hope that they are good enough to make Rangers the best team in Scotland. I'm not going to become obsessed with Celtic. There are seventeen teams in the First Division besides Rangers and if we are facing up to the new boys in the League, like Dumbarton say, then I'll be giving Dumbarton all my thoughts. I'll think about Celtic only when we are playing Celtic!

'I've always wanted to be a manager and I've never hidden that fact. Nor have I hidden the fact that this job, manager of Rangers, is the greatest job in the country. The job is new in that I have to make all the decisions . . . but the great thing is that nothing else has altered. I know the players. I have worked with them now for two years and we have been through a lot together in that time, including winning a European tournament. I know what they can do but we will be out to improve their game as much as possible. We won't be resting on any laurels we might have won in Barcelona. We will be looking for more success . . . that is the only way to be in this game.'

The Rangers' players will find that out, of course, as the Wallace way to success is unfolded for them. They will have some ideas of what they can expect from the tough talking,

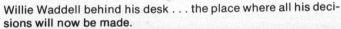

Willie Waddell behind his desk . . . the place where all his decisions will now be made.

hard driving man who is now the Boss on the training ground and in the dressing room. Wallace has never been a man to pull punches in any talk-ins with his players. Now, though, he has the full authority to back every word he utters.

Wallace is totally dedicated to football and to fitness. He thinks of little apart from the game and all that dedication will be essential to him as he fights to bring the Ibrox support the success they want at home to go with the new-found success they celebrated in Europe last season.

The fans want Rangers to be back at the top in Scotland. They don't want to play second fiddle to Celtic any longer than the seven years they have suffered as their greatest rivals have won one League title after another. Last season, after a disastrous start to the title race, and then a no-interest ending, Rangers finished up in third spot in the table, sixteen points behind Celtic. That has to be improved upon. . . .

But, apart from the Europe run, they had shown signs that they could become a major power again at home. They had a terrible opening to the season, losing three of their first four league games, to Partick Thistle, Celtic and Aberdeen. It was their worst-ever start to the League and it came on top of two defeats from Celtic in a League Cup section, defeats which

Rangers new manager Jock Wallace (centre) holds the European Cup Winners Cup and smokes a cigar in the dressing room after the game in Barcelona. Players in pic. are Dave Smith (left) Colin Stein and Willie Mathieson (right).

meant they had lost the trophy they had earned under Willie
Waddell's leadership the season before. The teams in Scotland refused to be impressed by these two fine pre-season wins
over Everton and Spurs. They lost again, to Hearts and to
Dundee before the end of October and then came the good
signs. Signs that gave hope to their fans. For, from then until
the spring they went from the bottom of the table to third
spot.

The one blemish in that long run was a defeat from
Celtic—their fourth of the season—by a last minute goal at
Celtic Park in January. The run brought them to a point
where they were challenging Aberdeen strongly for second
spot in the table . . . and then came that spell towards the end
of the season when Europe and the Scottish Cup assumed
more importance and League points were thrown away. In
that run, though, they had shown the same determination to
win as they had done in Europe and that was encouraging.

The Scottish Cup was expected to salve some of the hurt the
fans felt at the home failures. It might have done, too, but for
an injury to skipper John Greig in the first semi-final clash
with Hibs at Hampden. Rangers had reached the semi-finals
after a hard run in the competition. Their first match was

Rangers General Manager Willie Waddell (left) looks on as his
new Manager Jock Wallace (centre) plays the ball in this practice game. Player in pic. is Alex MacDonald.

13

After the Final whistle at Barcelona Stadium when Rangers
played Moscow Dynamo, Rangers player Jim Denny (left) looks
at his Manager Willie Waddell and coach Jock Wallace hug each
other after winning the tie.

away against Falkirk at Brockville. That was a draw
and Rangers won the Ibrox replay. Another away draw
followed, against Second Division St Mirren at Love Street,
but Rangers won this one easily. Then a third away game hit
them and it was a hard one. They were drawn to meet
Motherwell, who had just beaten them in a League game, and
that result meant that a needle game was to follow in the Cup.
The game at Fir Park finished in a draw and then Rangers
won the replay. That took them to the semi-final against Hibs.
Again there was a drawn first game . . . with John Greig being
badly injured in a tackle with Hibs' sweeper John Blackley.
Greig refused to leave the field that day, ignoring the
manager's instructions and eventually having his foot ban-
daged over his boot as he played on. The injury kept Greig out
for the rest of the season and his next full appearance was to
be in Barcelona

Without Greig's inspiration in the second game against
Hibs and with his replacement Derek Parlane suffering a
broken ankle, Rangers flopped to one of their poorest
performances of the season and were swept out of the Cup. It

was fortunate that the success in Europe was there for them . . . fortunate that the victory in Barcelona was achieved. Because that glory win meant that the fans were able to push the home failures to the backs of their minds.

It may not be so easy for them to do that again this season. Rangers' fans do not like to be reminded that Jock Stein's Celtic have won seven successive League titles. They want to see that championship flag flying over Ibrox once again. . . .

That must be Jock Wallace's main target in his new job. That must be the prize he hopes to win above all others. What he must hope is that the Barcelona win rids the players of the feeling they had that they have been jinxed when it came to winning the game's honours. That has hung around the club for some time. The players came so close, so often and then failed at the last gasp that some of them really believed that they were doomed to be the Rangers' team which had won less honours for the club than any other in history.

Barcelona has taken that worry from them—or it should have done! Now they have become the FIRST, in fact, the

Rangers General Manager Willie Waddell is seen drinking Champagne out of the European Cup Winners Trophy after the match in Barcelona.

ONLY, Rangers' team to win a major European trophy. That sends every one of these players into Ibrox legend. It will make their names rank with the greatest names from the glorious Ibrox past and that should help the new boss.

No one can write these players off now. No one can sneer at their achievements. And Jock Wallace takes over at a time when the players must be swelling with pride at what they accomplished in the season just past. He has to capitalise on these feelings of pride and he must try to channel them into positive aspects on the field of play, the one place to get the results that the fans will be looking for from him.

The way ahead is hard but Wallace is sufficiently realistic to know that for himself.

As for Willie Waddell, he has done what he set out to do two and a half years ago, when he accepted the job as manager. He wanted to bring pride back into the club. He wanted to restore their greatness and by becoming the first manager to guide them to victory in Europe he has done that. Now he moves into a new role, as the man in charge of the administrative side of the club. He will be successful here, too. To Waddell will fall the task of arranging the celebrations for the club centenary next year. And he will also become responsible for the proposed facelift at Ibrox.

All his long experience in the game will be used to further the greatness of the team he always refers to as 'The Rangers Football Club'. He will succeed in restoring their power in the game just as he succeeded in starting them off on the road to restoring their days of playing glory, too.

The Cup Winners Cup comes to Ibrox at last

by JOHN GREIG

There is no doubt in my mind that the moment I was presented with the European Cup Winners Cup deep in the heart of the giant Barcelona Stadium will remain the greatest of my football career. . . .

This was the moment that Rangers teams had waited for down through the years the club had battled in Europe . . . the moment that our huge and loyal support had dreamed of for the sixteen long years the club had competed in Europe. And I was lucky enough to be the first-ever Rangers' skipper to hold one of the Continent's major prizes.

Yet how we had to fight to earn that prize against a Russian team, Moscow Dynamo, who refused to give in at any stage of the match. I have never known as courageous a fight back as the one they staged against us on that memorable night in Spain. In a game which we believed we were going to win easily just after half time, a game which had gone exactly the way that we wanted it to go, we finished up fighting for our lives against a Russian team which was as talented as any European team I have ever played against. And braver than almost any other opponents I have been asked to face. . . .

What other team would go 3–0 down a few minutes after half time in a European tournament final and yet still keep fighting, still keep playing dangerous attacking football, and still be in with a chance of saving the game right up to the final whistle?

I cannot think of many . . . just as I could not believe that the Russians would be able to hit back at us with such power after we had scored that third goal in the final. I thought then that the game was finished and I said so to the rest of the team. I just could not see any team anywhere put us under pressure when we had reached such a commanding position in so important a game. I should have known better. I should have

17

remembered that we lost two goals to Sporting Club of Portugal in the same tournament at Ibrox earlier in the season . . . but I just did not see that happening again. I was wrong. . . .

You see, the game in Barcelona had progressed for us just as we had planned and hoped it would. In twenty four minutes Dave Smith had sent a perfectly flighted ball through the middle of the Russian defence. Our centre forward Colin Stein had chased it, got on the goal side of the defender who had been shadowing him and crashed a tremendous shot wide of the Russian goalkeeper Pilgui and into the net to put us into the lead. Five minutes before half time Dave moved cleverly out of defence once more to set up a second chance and a second goal.

This time he crossed perfectly into the Russian goalmouth. Willie Johnston rose as the Russian 'keeper hesitated for a split second and he placed his header out of the stranded Pilgui's reach and that meant we were two goals ahead.

We went in at half time holding that lead and yet, somehow, I found it difficult to grasp that we were really two goals in front.

The first half had been a bit nervous for both teams until we settled down a little with that first goal . . . and it had seemed to last an age. Although we had hoped for a half time lead I hadn't really expected to be two goals in front. I thought a single goal lead would be the best we could look for.

Then, when we scored that third goal in forty eight minutes, I was sure that, at last, we had clinched the European trophy we had wanted so desperately. Our giant goalkeeper Peter McCloy had sent one of his huge clearances soaring downfield. It went on and on and on, deceiving the bewildered Russian defenders, but not fooling Willie Johnston who had known what to expect! He went after the ball, brought it under control and then calmly placed it into the goal as the Russians scrambled to recover.

The fans on the terracings—and all of them seemed to be our fans—went delirious with joy and I think we were just as happy on the field. Never even in my most optimistic moments had I dreamed that we would reach such a commanding position in a European final. Maybe that's why I forgot about the Sporting Club match and about Mr Waddell's warning that the Russians would never give in. He had said that the Dynamo players would fight every inch of the way and that they would not stop fighting until the final whistle went. He was proved right. . . .

18

Rangers' skipper John Greig.

Skipper Greig in action during one of Rangers' big games last season.

And it didn't take so very long before the Russians proved him right . . . with most of their revival stemming from a substitution they made after fifty five minutes' play. That was when they sent on Estrokov for Jakubic. Now we had expected Estrokov to be on from the start, at outside right in place of Baidachnyi. Not that Baidachnyi had been unimpressive, for he had brought a lot of danger to us in the first half of the match when he twice set up chances, which luckily for us were missed by the other forwards. But, you see, Estrokov had been one of the players the Boss had seen in Moscow on his spy trip the previous week and he had been impressed. He had returned to warn us of both wingers, Estrokov and the outside left Evruzhikin.

Anyhow, ten minutes after half time Estrokov made his appearance to start taking on a roving role up front . . . and all our troubles began. We should have been able to coast along to an easy win. We should have been able to remain in control of the game, even with the Russians setting up most of the attacks. But it didn't happen the way it should have happened.

In sixty minutes after a defensive mistake—the nerves still hung around the players a little bit—Evruzhikin fastened onto the ball and hit it across goal. Estrokov was there to force the ball over the line and a minute later he almost did it again with a shot which raged just over our cross bar.

We were rattled by these two quick flashes from the substitute and we weren't helped any when the Russians mounted attack after attack to place us under as severe pressure as we had been under in Europe that season. Two minutes from the end the Russians broke through to score again, this time, through Makovikov. But that was too late for them to stage a rally to save the game . . . though I shudder to think of the strain we would have been under if that second goal had come earlier!

They were a tremendous team, well drilled and magnificently organised. And in Josef Sabo they had a wonderfully inspiring and influential player. He had lined up wearing the number nine jersey in a bid to complicate things for us, but he was playing in midfield and I had been given the job of marking him. It was a difficult task and I knew that. I had seen a lot of Sabo previously. During the World Cup in England in 1966, for example, I saw the Russians play several times and he had impressed me then. Now he is on the wrong side of thirty, classed as a veteran, but in my book after Barcelona he is still rated as one of the world's great players. In my career I have been asked to mark a lot of top class men and Sabo can hold his own with any of them. He was absolutely superb against us . . . and after trying to subdue him for that ninety minutes I know that better than anyone! He was everywhere in that final, pushing up with his forwards to start the moves which so often placed us in trouble, and back with his defence when they needed help.

Strangely enough, too, in spite of his age he just never seemed to tire. He kept going for the whole game and just as the Boss had said after seeing Dynamo in Moscow, Sabo was the man who made them play. It was probably because of his influence that Dynamo were less regimented than most Russian teams. With their organisation they combined a variety of flair in their play that is missing in most of the Russian teams I have had to face. So much so that I returned from Barcelona convinced that very soon one of the Russian club teams will make an impact in Europe by winning one of the major trophies.

I'm sure they must have thought they had a chance of beating us when things became so desperately close in that second half. I know that there were times when I began to think that we were going to be jinxed again, that we might only get a draw after the ninety minutes and then that we would lose the Cup in extra time. That last half hour of the game, after they had scored their first goal, was hell for me and the rest of the lads. And I know that the fans were suffering the same agonies as we were.

Then, suddenly, it was all over. The Spanish referee, Jose Ortiz de Mendibil, blew for time and the fans swamped us on the field. I was carried off to the dressing rooms by some of the supporters as they tried to stop me from being crushed by the thousands of fans who had invaded the field as they celebrated our victory. We did not know what happened after we were in the dressing rooms. We did not know that the police baton charged the crowd and that a battle broke out. We did not find out about that until much later.

The first hint we had had that there was trouble at all was when I had the Cup presented to me in private in a room under the stadium. I had hoped that I would be able to show the Cup to the fans who had travelled to Spain—all thirty thousand of them. But because of the after-match trouble I could not do that. Still, the fans knew that we had done the job we had come to Spain to do. They knew that after all these years of despair and disappointment the European Cup Win-

Rangers centre forward Colin Stein (left) throws his arms in the air after he had opened the scoring against Dynamo. The Dynamo defender on ground is Dolbonossov.

ners Cup was going to Glasgow to take pride of place in the Ibrox trophy room.

Now, even though I would not have said so at the time, I'm glad that there was a fight back by Dynamo. Glad because it helped to make the Final a memorable one. Much more memorable than the previous final appearance Rangers had made under my captaincy. That was in 1967 and it came the week after Celtic had beaten Inter Milan to win the European Cup in Lisbon.

That result placed an extra burden on us because everyone was wanting us to complete a great Glasgow double and stay upsides with our greatest football rivals. Yet, our game was in Nuremberg within easy reach of the fans of our opponents, Bayern Munich and the odds were stacked heavily against us. We eventually lost in extra time to a goal from Franz Roth in a

23

This sequence of seven photographs shows Willie Johnston's second goal against Moscow Dynamo in the Barcelona Stadium.

No. 1   Johnston outjumps the Dynamo defence in preparation for this cross ball.

No. 2   The ball speeds towards the net watched by Dalbonossov and Alex MacDonald. The other Dynamo player is Jukov. Pilgui the goalkeeper stands rooted as the ball passes him.

No. 3   The ball enters the net.

No. 4 Johnston and MacDonald throw their arms in the air after the ball hits the net.

No. 5 Johnston turns away after scoring.

No. 6 Alex MacDonald races after Johnston to congratulate him.

game which had been dull to play in and probably even duller to watch. Throughout the extra time period I had been praying that we would be able to get a replay and then in a second game both teams could provide the kind of game the fans expected. The kind of game they could look back on and remember with pride.

The whole of that match in Nuremberg seemed to be spent with the two teams sparring, feeling each other out and nervously trying to assess how the game should be played. In a second game that would not have been necessary. We would have been able to get down to the real business of playing and winning without delay.

The Barcelona, final, apart from an opening spell when nerves had a grip on both teams, was a far superior match. We played well and we scored our goals well in the earlier part of the match and then the Russians hurled themselves at us in the later stages and their efforts will never be forgotten by anyone who watched the match. My hope now is that the battle between the fans and the police which came afterwards won't cloud the fact that a great game had been played. The football was what we had all been in Barcelona for and that should not be forgotten by anyone.

It was upsetting to all of us that we were not presented publicly with the Cup . . . and it became even worse when we learned of the reasons why the trophy had to be presented privately.

But, I repeat, that sad aftermath to the game should not

No. 7   Johnston and MacDonald hug each other with delight.
        No. 9 is Colin Stein.

26

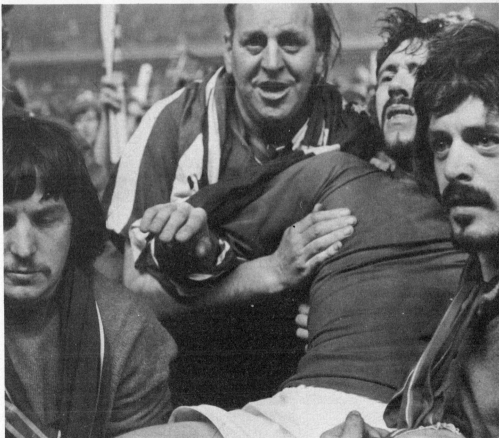

Willie Johnston (left) Rangers outside left drives the ball past Dynamo 'keeper Pilgui to score Rangers third goal. 27

Rangers captain John Greig is carried from the field by Fans after the game against Moscow Dynamo in Barcelona.

hide the fact that the 1972 European Cup Winners Cup Final between Rangers and Moscow Dynamo had been a game worthy of the occasion. It was not the tight and cautious final that fans are forced to watch so often now as two teams go into the game frightened of defeat.

Instead it was the kind of final where both teams went out to win by playing positive football. That's why it finished up with five goals being scored and with several other close things for the fans to talk about. The determination of both teams to win the game and to get goals gave Europe a football match to remember.

It was a more exciting final than that one in Nuremberg had been five years before . . . and not only because the result went the way I wanted it!

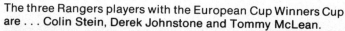
The three Rangers players with the European Cup Winners Cup are . . . Colin Stein, Derek Johnstone and Tommy McLean.

The Mischievous Monsieur Prouff

The troubled pattern that was to follow Rangers through their highly successful European Cup Winners Cup campaign was surely set by the first round match against the French Cup holders Rennes. . . .

And the problem that haunted that opening tie began before a ball had been kicked. It began, in fact, when Ibrox boss Willie Waddell made a spy dash to Brittany to see the Frenchmen in action just a few days before the Scottish season was due to open. I was with Waddell when he went to see Rennes play Bastia in a French First Division game. He saw his future opponents win 1–0 after they had been defied for most of the game by a goalkeeper well known to Glasgow fans, the Yugoslav international Ilya Pantelic who had played for Vojvodina, Novi Sad against both Rangers and Celtic in European games. At one time he had impressed both members of the Old Firm and had almost signed for Celtic. Now he was in France, playing for Bastia and playing quite magnificently. Indeed it took a penalty to beat him and give Rennes their victory.

He was the star of the game and ironically the problem that Waddell met up with came from two more Yugoslavs, two players who had just been signed by the manager of Rennes, Jean Prouff.

That night in the Parc des Sports they sat immediately behind Waddell and myself in the Rennes' directors' box. They were both Yugoslav international players, a midfield man Kobechek from Vardar and a striker Mojsov from Dinamo Zagreb. They had just joined the French club and Jean Prouff insisted that both would be eligible for the games against Rangers. We doubted that because of the strict registration rules which govern the two major European tournaments. When we arrived back in Glasgow and checked with the European Union headquarters in Berne the doubts we had seemed well founded. Neither player appeared to have clearance from their home association in Belgrade and that meant they were ruled out of the first round tie.

Eventually after a long drawn-out wrangle which lasted until the eve of the first game in Rennes the European Union decreed that one of the players, the striker Mojsov, was allowed to play. The registration difficulties kept Kobechek out of the games against the Scots.

Apart from these off-field problems Waddell had seen danger on the field from the Frenchmen in that spy trip game. Team boss Prouff had been around European football for a long time and his non-stop stream of propaganda proved that. He had managed Standard Liege when they defeated Rangers in the European Cup many years before . . . now he was happily forecasting a double against the Ibrox team.

And his hopes were based on a brilliant young midfield man Raymond Keruzore, a man Waddell likened to Jim Baxter at his peak. That was high praise and the way Keruzore combined in midfield with the veteran French international Andre Betta spelled danger to Rangers' hopes of a long run in the tournament. After watching the game against Bastia Waddell was high in his praise of the French team and was feted on champagne by the town mayor who, like the rest of the town, was proud of the club's Breton background.

When Jean Prouff appeared at Ibrox to watch Rangers against Celtic—a game the Ibrox team lost—he was as polite as Waddell had been in France. He called the Old Firm clash one of the 'world's great games' and insisted that it was no disgrace for any team to lose to Celtic on the day. He added that Rangers might have too much power and too much skill for his own team. At that time it looked as if only the registration wrangle would bring trouble to the tie. But those of us who felt that way were soon to be proved wrong. The mischievous Monsieur Prouff was to show us that immediately following the first leg of the first round tie in France . . . and mainly because Rangers had gone to the Parc des Sports and held Rennes to a 1–1 draw. It was exactly the result that Waddell had wanted . . . but naturally it did not suit Jean Prouff or any of his players!

In fact, it was a notable and important result for Rangers. They had had a disastrous start to the League programme at home, one that had them still pointless when they travelled to France to take on Rennes who were lying joint third in the

es defender Chlosta heads the ball away as Colin Stein
jers) runs in.

French First Division after a series of good results.

Because of the circumstances Waddell was forced to go to Rennes to play the game tight. It is always an understandable tactic when playing away from home in European competitions, but this time it was even more understandable when Rangers' League record was examined! It was hard to believe that a team which had looked so packed with power and so determined to gain success should slump so badly and Waddell was as worried over the form mystery as anyone else. The match against the Frenchmen was a chance to rebuild their shattered confidence if only a good result could be obtained. It would also, of course, give them the chance to stay in Europe instead of being forced out in the first round as they had been the previous season in the Fairs Cup clash against old rivals Bayern Munich. A great deal depended on that game in the picturesque Parc des Sports. . . .

31

Rangers outside forward Willie Henderson is tackled by Rennes defender Chlosta.

Because of that the natural attacking instincts of the Ibrox team were curbed on Waddell's instructions. Caution was demanded . . . and caution became the main tactic. In midfield Alex MacDonald and skipper John Greig were handed the marking roles against the men who had impressed Waddell when he watched Rennes.

MacDonald snapped terrier-like at the heels of the elegant Raymond Keruzore while the power of Greig subdued the wily veteran Andre Betta. They were the play-makers of the Rennes team and they were effectively taken out of the game by the Rangers' tactics. Watched by eighteen thousand fans who were there to welcome European football back to Brittany after several years' absence the Scots did the destroying job they had been asked to do. It was not pretty to watch . . . but it was effective. With Keruzore and Betta struggling the Rangers' defence then used long balls to set away their strikers and catch Rennes on the break. It was another tactic that worked when speed ace Willie Johnston put them in the lead in sixty-eight minutes and when Tommy McLean had another chance but missed.

Eventually ten minutes from the end the French substitute Redon equalised but with away goals counting double in European competition Rangers were already ahead in the game and that was the important thing for the Ibrox men. It was not seen that way, though, by Prouff. The French team boss, tagged a soccer idealist by the local pressmen, tried to live up to that image with a bad tempered blast at Rangers, Waddell and the tactics they had employed to frustrate his team. The politeness had vanished. The bottles of champagne which had welcomed us on the spy trip were not uncorked. Prouff had abandoned diplomacy. Now he wanted only to make mischief.

Icily he told me after the game: 'That was not football that Rangers played against us tonight. That was not the game of football as I know it or as my players know it, or as our supporters know it. What the Scottish players did tonight had nothing to do with football. It was anti-football. They came here only to stop us playing instead of trying to play themselves. All Brittany is angry at the way this game was played. We will come to Glasgow in two weeks and when we are there we will show how football should be played. We believe that skill is more important than results. Winning a European tie is not as important to me as playing attractive football. . . .'

Clearly Prouff was attempting by these insults to rile Rangers, to drag Willie Waddell into a war of words and then to annoy the Rangers' players so much that they would attack recklessly in the second leg at Ibrox. In both attempts he failed. A laughing Waddell told me on the flight home: 'I'd be a lot more worried right now if Mr Prouff was being pleasant about me. Because if he was handing out praise then it would be because he had won the game. If he had been friendly after the game then we would have been the team behind the eight ball for the second leg game. Instead it's his team who are in that position and if he comes to Ibrox to show us how to play then he'll have to go some. We are in the commanding position in this tie and we intend to stay that way.'

33

Willie Johnston (Rangers) stands over Rennes goalkee
Aubour as Cosnard (Rennes) looks on.

The only unhappy thing for Rangers from that first leg game was that three of their players were booked by a fussy Austrian referee. Willie Johnston, Ronnie McKinnon and Jim Denny who had come on as a late substitute were the three who were cautioned. Young Denny was the unluckiest of the trio. He had been pulled up for offside as he went through but played the ball just as the whistle blew. It was an instinctive reaction . . . but enough for the Austrian to caution him for time-wasting!

Still, the bookings were a minor blot on the Rangers' result . . . and the Prouff outpourings were a minor irritant though he did keep up a non-stop stream of propaganda when he brought his team to Glasgow for the second leg game. In his hotel just a few hundred yards from Ibrox, Prouff held a press conference when he did his best to annoy Rangers.

'Rangers lost to Aberdeen on Saturday so the problems for this game clearly lie with them,' he observed.

'We will win this game because my players have more skill than Rangers who rely only on power,' he claimed.

'No matter what happens in the game Rennes will remain a credit to football as always,' he insisted.

'To win the tie may be important . . . but to play well and to attack is even more important,' he declared.

And, then, with a final piece of mischief-making he shrugged and commented: 'After all I will not lose my job if we lose this tie because my club are not a club who would do such a thing to a manager.'

All of Prouff's remarks were aimed at upsetting Rangers. They were done in a bid to goad Rangers into ignoring defence and hurling themselves forward into undisciplined attacks which would leave gaps in their defence. Prouff was hoping that the Ibrox team would fall into the trap he was carefully laying for them with the non-stop stream of words flowing from his hotel.

Certainly Rangers had lost 2-0 to Aberdeen on the previous Saturday and had remained far too close to the bottom of the First Division for a team of their standing while Rennes had forced themselves into second spot behind Marseilles in the French First Division. Although the Rangers' position was a false one—and was very soon to be proved so—it still existed and the pressure was on the Scots. The wily Prouff knew that, hence the extra pressures he was trying to create.

But it was not to help him any once the playing started. Forty-two thousand fans were at Ibrox to see Rangers, with Willie Henderson back at outside right for his first full game of the season, make the talkative Frenchman eat his words. Rangers allied common sense with caution in their attacks and in thirty-eight minutes they scored the goal that gave them victory over the French side. Willie Johnston beat two French defenders and then saw his shot pushed out by the French international goalkeeper Marcel Aubour. It went only as far as little Alex MacDonald who slammed the ball into the net. It was the only goal of the game and scant reward for the effort Rangers put into the match.

Henderson and Johnston on the wings were the stars of the

game and Aubour had to make daring saves from both in the second half when Colin Stein also hit the bar. That is how much Rangers were on top and for all Prouff's talk of attack the Frenchmen were lined up in a 4–4–2 formation and used the offside trap almost incessantly to stop the Rangers' raids. After the game Prouff admitted: 'Rangers were the better team and Rangers deserved to win. They showed more class, more skill tonight especially on the wings where Henderson and Johnston were outstanding.' Then, in a final barb which he obviously could not resist he added: 'It is only a pity that our fans in France were not able to see Rangers play in this way. . . .'

But by this time Rangers had ceased to care what Mr Prouff thought about them or about their tactics. Because Rangers had won and Europe was bringing them solace for the League disappointments they had been forced to suffer at home in Scotland. They might be languishing in a position near the bottom of the First Division but they were still competing in the European Cup Winners Cup.

As Willie Waddell admitted to me the next day in his office

Rennes Goalkeeper Aubour dives at the feet of Rangers outside forward Willie Henderson.

at Ibrox: 'We had to get a result in that game. It was vital to the team to stay in Europe, to keep the interest going in the Continental games and, just as important, to give us a boost for the league here at home.

'There was a double edge to our game against the French. We had to win it for the two reasons and Prouff knew that. He realised that the pressure was on us even though we did have the advantage after getting a draw with them over in France. He wanted us to go helter skelter into attack against his team. He tried to get us angry enough to forget all about defence and in a two-legged tie in Europe that just cannot be done. Despite everything that he was saying we were already winning the tie when he brought his team to Glasgow and we weren't going to lose sight of that for one moment. We had to approach the game with calmness and with a great deal of caution and we did that. I was very pleased indeed about the way the players approached this match. They worked hard in both games and in each one we got the result that we wanted. Rennes were no pushovers as their own league record shows. And it was a match we simply had to win. There is no doubting that.'

Waddell's players had rewarded him with the performance and with the result he had wanted. Rangers had gone through to the second round of the European Cup Winners Cup and that was what he had wanted so very much. The tie had been a difficult one, especially when first round draws can on occasions be so very much easier. Now he hoped for an easy break in the second round. . . .

But it was not to be. A few days later the draw was made and Rangers were paired with the favourites for the trophy and former winners Sporting Club of Portugal.

The European problems persisted. . . .

Experiments in Sweden

Rangers' Manager Willie Waddell is not given to the idea of allowing his players to spend their pre-season on a casual build-up to what lies ahead of them. When Rangers go abroad they go to work and to learn and last year's trip to Sweden was no exception. . . .

In fact, if any of the players had the idea that they were setting off on a holiday jaunt it was killed by Waddell immediately he stepped on the jet which took them to their training camp near Gothenburg. It was on that flight that Waddell laid things on the line for all his players. He made it clear that the team was going to Sweden to work. And to work hard. Then he underlined the fact by announcing publicly that not a single man on the Rangers' playing staff could be guaranteed a first team place because of past performances. That place could only be earned by top class displays every week. . . .

As we flew to Copenhagen on the first leg of the journey I sat with Waddell on the plane as he told me: 'Big names and big money mean nothing to me. I want men in the team who will give everything they have got for me and for Rangers. I will not tolerate players who simply want to coast along week after week. The past does not count and reputations won't impress me any when it comes to naming my first team over here in Gothenburg. I decided to take this trip because it gives us the chance to work hard at the game.

'There were dozens of opportunities to take holiday trips but they don't interest me because they would not be to Rangers' benefit. Last year we went to West Germany and we went there looking for a team, trying to find a recognised first team. This season I am setting out with several alternative teams in mind. This is a chance to try out various formations that have suggested themselves to me and they will be tested in a competitive atmosphere.'

Jock Wallace (centre) Rangers' Trainer, is seen taking part in the training session with the players at the Albion.

On that last point there was no doubt. Rangers had been asked to take part in a four club tournament in Gothenburg. Their opponents were two local clubs, Orgryte, who were skippered by former Rangers' star Orjan Persson, and GAIS, and English First Division side Wolves.

Waddell had decided to base his team at the Hindas training camp some thirty miles outside the city. It was a camp made famous in 1958 when Brazil used it as their headquarters when they won the World Cup and Wolves, too, had elected to stay there. It was a splendidly equipped camp and one that suited coach Jock Wallace—a fitness fanatic—down to the ground. It was the ideal setting for Wallace as he hammered the players to the peak of fitness he demanded. There were few distractions, only the thickly wooded hills and the ice cold lake.

I still remember the first training session the players had there, stripped to the waist in the warm sunshine they went through their paces watched by several of the Wolves' stars.

I sat by the side of the training pitch with two of the English club's Scots' stars, inside forward Jim McCalliog and centre half Francis Munro. McCalliog admitted to me: 'I haven't seen any team look as fit as the Rangers' lads look. We are supposed to be fit but they're ahead of us. They look so fast and so strong. . . I just hope that we don't have to meet them in the tournament.'

At that time a clash between the two British sides looked certain. The tournament was arranged so that Wolves played Orgryte in the opening match, the following night Rangers met GAIS, the next night the two losing teams from the first matches met to settle the third place and then the final was played on the fourth night. The Swedish organisers were hoping that Rangers and Wolves would be the the teams in the final. But, as so often happens in football, things did not work out as everyone expected. For Rangers, the team who had impressed everyone who had watched their public work outs fell at the very first hurdle against the Swedish Second Division Leaders GAIS.'

In a quite astonishing game the Scots were trailing 2–0, fought back to be ahead 3–2 and then were sensationally robbed of victory when the Swedes scored twice in the last five minutes. As Waddell had hinted big name stars had been axed for the game. The men who were dropped were Willie Henderson, replaced by close-season signing Tommy McLean and Colin Stein whose centre forward spot was taken

Tommy McLean does some exercises in the Rangers' gym.   41 over by teenage wonder boy Derek Johnstone.

Rangers went behind to a penalty kick in five minutes and then to add to their worries debut man Tommy McLean missed a penalty when the star of the Swedish side, goalkeeper Benny Larsson, saved his kick. In fifty-three minutes Rangers went two goals down and then, suddenly, they began to play the way everyone had expected. Derek Johnstone, Alfie Conn and Willie Johnston all scored to make it 3–2 and the small group of fans who had followed them from Scotland were chanting their victory slogans. But in eighty five minutes GAIS were awarded their second penalty of the game, scored from it, and in the last minute snatched an amazing winner when one of their forwards beat Peter McCloy with an over head kick.

As Wolves' midfield general McCalliog summed it up going out of the stand—'It was an injustice for Rangers to be beaten that way. No one should be able to score lucky goals like that last one. Any other time he would have missed the ball altogether.'

Rangers knew that as well as anyone but the goal counted and the defeat meant they had to play their second match twenty four hours later against the First Division team Orgryte who had lost narrowly to Wolves in the tournament opener. The Swedes were determined to make it hard for Rangers, especially ex-Ibrox man Orjan Persson who had played for Sweden in the 1970 World Cup.

Waddell produced another team shake-up for this second game. Centre half Ronnie McKinnon went out and Jim Denny was drafted into the back four to play alongside Colin Jackson at the heart of the defence. Alfie Conn dropped out and so did Derek Johnstone who was injured. Willie Henderson returned to play on the left wing with Colin Stein back at centre. It was a game that saw bookings for McLean and Stein, a game that was scarred by trouble and had the local referee call the team captains, John Greig and Persson together in a bid to stop the violence.

Rangers had started the game as if they would win easily with John Greig scoring in just twenty five seconds. Then in forty eight minutes Tommy McLean scored his first goal for Rangers and that meant that the consolation prize of third place—a prize that Rangers had little use for—had been clinched. The Swedes did score a goal before the end but Rangers playing their second match in twenty four hours were carried through by their remarkable fitness... though at

considerable cost. The bad-tempered game brought them
seven injuries, all of which needed treatment the next day at
Hindas. Eventually Wolves won the tournament, surprising
even themselves. . . because they had feared the challenge and
power of the Scots more than anything else. And they
admitted as much at the celebration banquet when the trophy
was presented.

Rangers remained at Hindas for a few days and then to
conclude their Swedish stay they moved down to the tiny port

Orjan Persson, former Ranger and now with Orgryte of Sweden.   43

of Haelsingborg just across the straits from Denmark. It was a beautiful spot and a pleasant setting for Rangers to regain the winning touch that had been expected in their disappointing first game. The training sessions at Hindas were now beginning to pay off. The players looked fit and purposeful. More than that even they looked hungry for games and hungry, too, for success. This was the attitude that Waddell had wanted to instil in them from the start of the trip.

It was a quaint little ground with almost a village green atmosphere with flags flying from the tiny stand and the inevitable Rangers' supporter with his Union Jack in the crowd. How the fans reach these unknown spots remains a constant mystery to all of us who have travelled with the club over the years. No matter where Rangers play someone is there to cheer them on.

Haelsingborg was no different and this time there was plenty of reason for the lone fan to cheer on his heroes. This game was the Swedish pay off for Waddell and his right hand man, coach Jock Wallace. This was the night the team were on song after the eight days of hard work at Hindas. With both Stein and Derek Johnstone missing because of injuries it meant Rangers going into the game without their main strikers. Goals could have been hard to come by. . . instead they arrived with ease.

Inside five minutes—the most blistering start I can remember to any game—Rangers had two goals disallowed, missed two easy chances and scored one goal through Alex MacDonald. And things didn't just peter out after that fantastic opening. Before the game was over Alfie Conn had scored twice and John Greig had added a fourth. After the game the tour organiser, Borje Lantzke, a Swede who now stays in Cascais near Lisbon, told me he had never seen football like it. If Rangers had not won the trophy in Gothenburg they had, at least won friends in Sweden by their displays.

Following that last match Lantzke told me: 'Rangers are wonderful ambassadors for Scottish football. I couldn't be happier with the way they performed. OK, so they did not win the Gothenburg tournament but in the long run that did not matter as far as I was concerned. What counted with me was the way that they played. They are the kind of team who give value for money. They do not simply go through the motions in games that might not matter. . . they play full out all the time and this is important to me. Haelsingborg is a small

44   Rangers new close season signing Tommy McLean is seen running round these obstacles during a training session at the Albion.

town and they do not get the chance to see top teams in action so very often. The display that Rangers provided will be remembered here for many, many years.

Rangers simply do not let the public down in any game they play. As far as I am concerned I would put them on tour again any time they wanted to get away from Scotland.

'It could be that opportunities will present themselves either here or in other countries next season and I will be trying to arrange something. Rangers will do nothing but good for Scottish football. . . believe me because I know. Too often teams have let me down. That can never be said about Rangers.'

It was an unsolicited tribute from the vastly experienced Lantzke, a man who has handled so many of the top teams

Derek Johnstone is seen doing exercises in the Rangers' gym.

from Europe and from South America too. And it was a tribute that Rangers had earned the hard way. They had lost the Gothenburg tournament they had wanted so much to win but for Waddell the disappointment had been lessened by the performances from his team after that shock opener. Then it had been lessened still further by the reaction of the Swedish hosts to the displays of his team and the performances of his players.

Also he had been able to experiment as he had wanted to do. He had made it clear that no one's first team place was automatic and he had seen Sandy Jardin, a leg break victim at the end of the previous season, come back to international form.

The time in Sweden had not been wasted. . . .

Rangers young centre forward Derek Johnstone is seen leaping over these small obstacle fences at the Albion training ground.

The Lisbon Story

In all the years I have been jetting around the world with Rangers I have never known a more nerve-shattering and dramatic trip than the one to Lisbon last season for the second leg second round match in the European Cup Winners Cup. . . .

The clash with Sporting Club of Portugal, one time holders of the trophy and one of the great names in European soccer, eventually brought in its wake a controversy which convulsed European football. But that all came at the end of the story after the second game in Lisbon early in November. . . .

The Lisbon story, in fact, had started at the end of October with a first half of astonishing football from Rangers at Ibrox. There were fifty thousand fans there that night to see the Portuguese who had come with a high reputation. The spy trip preliminaries had been duly completed and Ibrox boss Willie Waddell had returned from Lisbon to warn his team that Sporting Club had more skilful players and looked even more dangerous opponents than the Frenchmen of Rennes had looked in the opening round.

Meanwhile, Sporting Club boss, the dapper little Fernando Vaz who had at one time been Portugal's national team boss, had come to Ibrox and told us that, he feared 'Rangers' power play'.

Inside half an hour little Vaz had his worries confirmed . . . not by power, mind you, but by some of the finest football Rangers had played that season.

Sporting Club did have an impressive line-up, a team littered with Portuguese international players, a dusky star from Brazil in Chico and a highly priced Argentinian centre forward in Hector Yazalde. Yazalde was the man Waddell rated above all the others. . . .

But, in spite of their stars, Sporting Club were destroyed in

Rangers inside forward Alfie Conn (right) lectures Lisbon's No. 13 Gomesz as Alec MacDonald (left Rangers) looks on.

49

that first half, though, to be fair, few teams would have lived with Rangers in that form. Three gloriously worked free kick moves, two of them playing on a weakness of the Portuguese goalkeeper for high cross balls, brought the Scots a 3–0 lead inside half an hour. They scored first in nine minutes when Andy Penman cleverly flighted in a free kick which Damas mistimed and Colin Stein headed into the net. A couple of minutes later Penman was injured and had to limp off to be replaced by Alfie Conn. It didn't upset Rangers' rhythm any. In twenty minutes from another free kick in almost the same position as the first brought goal number two. This time Dave Smith swung the ball into goal, Damas missed it completely, and Stein was there to finish it off again. Eight minutes after that Alfie Conn slipped a short free kick to Willie Henderson as the Sporting Club defenders looked for another high lob. The little winger cut in quickly, reached the edge of the box and hammered a tremendous shot into the net. It was a fantastic goal to crown that fantastic first half hour. The crowd were going wild with delight and, really, Rangers should have been further ahead than just by the three goals they had scored.

Sporting Club did not seem able to live with them and the unfortunate goalkeeper Damas was having a nightmare match. He had been the same a week earlier playing for Portugal against Scotland at Hampden. His poor judgment of cross balls had been noted then by Rangers and they had played on that weakness to perfection.

But, just as the second leg in Lisbon was beginning to look like a formality, Rangers slipped up. Probably because of over-confidence—and after the first half it was hard to blame them for feeling that—they relaxed their grip on the game. They lost a little in midfield, and they relaxed fatally in defence. Because of this the Portuguese were able to score twice in the second half to send the crowd home stunned in disbelief. Chico got the first in seventy minutes and Pedro Gomesz snatched the second nine minutes from the end. It was hard for the fans to believe the score as they trooped silently into the night from the Ibrox terracings. Instead of their team being in total command of the situation and heading for an easy second leg trip to Lisbon they were now balanced on the precipice of a one goal lead.

The next morning at Ibrox manager Willie Waddell maintained that his team could still reach the quarter finals. He pointed out that they should have been five goals ahead at

50   The kind of hard work that faces veteran centre half Ronnie McKinnon who broke his leg in the game against Sporting Club of Portugal. This will be his hard road back to fitness. . . .

half time and I agreed with that. But, in spite of it all, knowing the difficulties of any game in Lisbon I found it hard to see them crashing through to the next round.

And the chirpiness of little Fernando Vaz didn't reassure me any. Grinningly he admitted: 'We should be out of the tournament after the way that Rangers played in the first half . . . but we are not. Rangers were truly magnificent. Playing that way they would be among the best in Europe.'

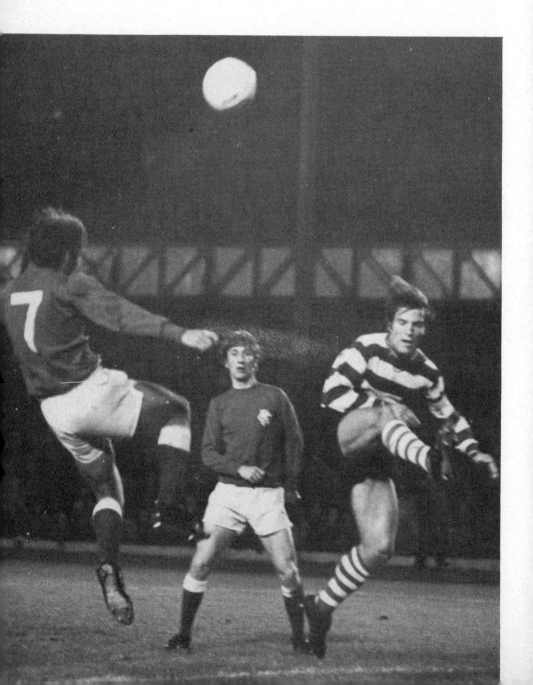

Then he added: 'Now, though, we are brought back to life because of the two goals we were able to get in the second half. We need just one more goal in Lisbon and we are through and I am sure that we will get that goal. And possibly more. . . .'

The euphoria which had surrounded Rangers' first half performance had vanished and in the last League game before they flew out for the Portuguese capital it seemed that their chances had been hit still further. They met Kilmarnock in a tough game which they won 3–1 but at the expense of having right back Sandy Jardine ordered off and left back Willie Mathieson taken to hospital for chest X-rays after getting a nasty rib knock. It was not the happiest Rangers' party which met that Monday morning at Abbotsinch Airport and their gloom was soon to be deepened.

This time the dark mood of gloom which settled around the party had nothing to do with injuries or even football. It stemmed from a strike of luggage porters at London Airport which was supposed to be the first stop for us on our way to Lisbon.

We were delayed for several hours at Glasgow before take off for London. Then in the afternoon at Heathrow we were told that there was no way for the team to reach Lisbon by scheduled flights. So, instead of a jet to Lisbon and a short bus journey to the team's head-quarters at the millionaires' playground of Estoril, we made a trek across London by coach to Stansted Airport where Manager Willie Waddell had managed after great difficulty to arrange a charter flight. But at midnight we were still at Stansted after a travelling day that had lasted almost twenty hours for some of the players . . . and now the charter had been postponed until the following morning.

We booked into various local hotels and then headed for Stansted again in the morning. Eventually at six-thirty on the day before the game Rangers dragged themselves wearily into their hotel at Estoril. It was just twenty-seven hours before kick-off time and it had been a dreadful build-up to the big game . . . but bravely Willie Waddell refused to make excuses.

'Listen,' he told me, 'we won't be hiding behind any delays or travel hold-ups. We are making no complaints and certainly no excuses whatsoever. We have a job to do and the only way is to get on with it. There is no use moping around. Our players are fit enough to get over this all right. And they will do it, too.'

Waddell was right and he was proved right in one of

Rangers outside forward Willie Henderson (No. 7) and Lisbon defender Carlos jump to head this cross ball. Rangers player looking on, centre, is Graham Fyfe.

European football's most sensational nights. I doubt if I shall
ever forget that night in the Jose d'Alvalade Stadium. It was a
night of drama and of tragedy, of chaos and of confusion and
eventually of triumph for the brave Scots. A triumph that, at
first, they did not even realise they had gained!

There were sixty thousand fans in Sporting Club's Stadium,
crowding forward on to the touchlines and setting off

54   Colin Stein (left Rangers) heads the ball past Lisbon's keeper
Damas to score a goal.

interminable rockets as they urged their team forward for the single goal needed to take them through. Trumpets blasted and drums beat out Latin rhythms as a salute to the Sporting goal when it arrived in twenty-five minutes when Yazalde put them in front. Just one minute later they were silenced again when Colin Stein snatched the equaliser.

It soon became clear that Rangers had not come solely committed to defence. They had come hoping to score vital away goals—the goals which count double in the event of a draw in the two-legged European ties. In fact when Tome scored a second for Sporting Club in thirty-eight minutes Rangers still kept moving forward trying to find the gaps they needed. . . .

One minute after half time the gap appeared and that man Stein, the hammer of the Portuguese in this tie, was there to level the second leg scores yet again. Now the Scots in the crowd realised their team was in with a fantastic chance.

Then tragedy struck in seventy-two minutes when centre half Ronnie McKinnon went down with a broken leg after he had been fouled. Although all the players had heard the crack of the leg breaking as McKinnon went down the Dutch referee Laurens van Raavens—later to be the villain of the whole piece—waved play on for several minutes before deciding to wave on the Rangers' trainer. McKinnon was carried off on a stretcher, and taken to a local hospital while Dave Smith slotted in alongside Colin Jackson in the re-organised defence.

Still, in spite of all the problems it looked as if the Scots would hold out. But three minutes from time Pedro Gomesz scored a third for Sporting Club. The tie was now deadlocked with the teams level on aggregate with both having scored the same number of away goals even, and so the game moved into extra time. Rangers looked stronger now, even with all the exhausting travel they had faced, than their Portuguese rivals. And their superior fitness told when Willie Henderson put them in front in the first half of extra time. Five minutes from the end though the ill luck which had dogged the team since flying out of Glasgow struck again. Colin Jackson handled the ball in the penalty box, a penalty was given and Peres scored. That was when the trouble really started. . . .

The teams were again level on aggregate, But Rangers had scored one more away goal and should automatically have qualified. But the tall Dutch referee decided that away goals scored in extra time did not count double and so ordered

56

Colin Stein (Rangers, not in picture) shot is net-bound to score a goal for Rangers. Alex MacDonald (centre Rangers) follows the ball into the net. Lisbon players Carlos (No. 6) and Larenjeira look on.

penalty kicks to be taken to decide the tie.

Incredibly Rangers missed four out of the scheduled five kicks, obviously with the players totally disheartened by the referee's decision which seemed to have robbed them of the tie. And they were also intimidated by the crowd which had flooded over the terracing walls to pack the touchlines.

The Rangers' misses—Sporting Club meanwhile were scoring with their kicks—meant that the Portuguese team were in front on penalties and their fans swarmed on to the field to carry off their heroes. Rangers, drooping with despair made wearily for their own dressing room convinced that they had been beaten. . . .

In the Press Box perched high over the stadium we remained convinced that the referee had blundered and that Rangers were through to the quarter finals before the penalty taking farce was staged. One of my colleagues, John Mackenzie of the *Scottish Daily Express*, was particularly adamant. He had consulted the rule governing this aspect of the tournament just a few days before leaving Glasgow. Now he was in no doubt that Rangers were the winners. There was confusion everywhere but, immediately, pressmen not involved with phoning stories at the time dashed to the Rangers' dressing room to tell Ibrox boss Willie Waddell.

The players were sitting around the dressing-room slumped in despondency until the news was broken. Then Waddell dashed along the corridor, clutching a copy of the UEFA rules, to see the neutral observer from the European Union. This official of the organising body was then called on to make a ruling. After long talks in private Waddell eventually emerged from the meeting to announce that Rangers were indeed through to the quarter finals and that the referee had made a mistake. . . .

Meanwhile in Glasgow my office had telephoned Dr Hans Bangerter, general secretary of UEFA to ask for his ruling. It was simple and it was direct and it said quite categorically—'Rangers have won. The referee is completely in error. It used to be that away goals did not count double during extra time but that rule was changed and the referee should have known that.'

It was two o'clock in the morning before Rangers finally knew for certain that they were through, although the referee Laurens van Raavens stalked in icy silence from his dressing-room refusing to answer any questions from Scottish pressmen.

Planeloads of Rangers' fans meantime had left for home believing that their team was out of Europe and thousands of Portuguese were celebrating in the bars of Lisbon believing that their team was in the quarter finals. It was a mad, mad, night in Lisbon. An unforgettable night!

The following day angry Sporting Club officials flew to Switzerland to plead their team's case but the rules were clear and their journey was a wasted one. Rangers had triumphed and the fact that technically—the away goals counting double rule had clinched the win—it was a rule book victory did not detract one bit from the display they had given.

It was a display of character and courage, two of the qualities in their play which were to be seen again and again in their march through Europe. They had arrived just a little more than twenty-four hours before the game as tired as any team I can remember after a nightmare journey from Glasgow. Then they had gone about the game as if they were simply refusing to acknowledge the possibility of defeat from the classy Portuguese. Even the loss of that experienced centre half star Ronnie McKinnon failed to damp the spirit of these Rangers' players.

As Manager Waddell admitted afterwards: 'I couldn't have been more proud of the way these lads worked out there in that match. They gave absolutely everything they had. If they had lost that game then it would have been one of the greatest injustices in European football.'

'The one saddening aspect is that Ronnie should have broken his leg so tragically. I feel upset for him . . . but for the rest there is only the highest of praise.'

It was praise that Waddell was soon to get used to handing out in Europe. . . .

Spying in Europe

by JOCK WALLACE

I find it almost impossible to say just how important a spy mission into Europe can be to any team taking part in one of the three Continental tournaments. It is a job that cannot be over-estimated because it provides a club with a chance to assess just where the main problems will lie when you must face the other team in the actual games. . . .

If you are unable to fit in a spy trip, and that can happen occasionally because of crowded fixture lists, then you find that a lot of time must be spent on the field in a kind of soccer sparring in the opening stages of the match. That part of the game has to be used as a kind of feeling-out process for all the players. They might have no knowledge of the general tactical formation of the opposition or of the individual players' traits and abilities. A spy trip can bring you all of these details and the Boss (Manager Willie Waddell) has insisted almost always that someone makes this 007 journey into Europe before all our games. It falls to either himself or to me to do the job.

Last season, for instance, a few days before we were set to play Bayern Munich in the semi-final first leg of the European Cup Winners Cup I found myself in West Germany. I was there to watch a German Cup game where Bayern were facing Cologne in the first leg of a quarter final game on their own ground in Munich.

Bayern won that game easily by 3–0 and as I sat in the stand at the Grunwalder Stadium I saw them parade all their style. They were a formidable team, but that was something I had known when I had set out from Glasgow to watch them. I had known it from the reputation they had built up in West Germany, from the international stature of their top players, and because the Boss had been to see them a week or two earlier against Stuttgart. Their team contained six of the current

West German international team who were to beat England just a month or so after I saw them. They were the two pin up boys of West German football, sweeper Franz Beckenbauer and centre forward Gerd Muller, plus goalkeeper Sepp Maier, left back Paul Breitner, centre half George Schwarzenbeck and inside left Uli Hoeness.

Their reputation was frightening and against Cologne they lived up to it. . . .

Mind you, all the way through the Cup Winners Cup tournament last season there had been a strong feeling amongst the boys that if we were to win the trophy then at some stage we would have to beat Bayern. When we drew them in the semi-finals there was a sense of inevitability about the whole thing . . . almost as if the lads knew they were fated to meet

Jock Wallace, Rangers' manager, the man who spotted a flaw 61 in Beckenbauer's make-up—'He could be pressured into mistakes'.

them again. The teams' paths had crossed twice before. In Nuremberg in the Cup Winners Cup Final of 1967 when Bayern beat Rangers 1–0 after extra time and the other season in the Fairs Cup when we lost 1–0 to them in Munich and drew 1–1 at Ibrox to go out in the first round.

We had drawn at Ibrox only because of the brilliant form of Sepp Maier. He defied us that night and more than anyone else had been responsible for knocking us out of Europe. . . .

Anyhow, all of that was going through my mind as I sat in the stand at Munich waiting for the game to begin. I was looking for some chink in Bayern's armour, some little flaw which we could exploit when it came to the time to play them. My normal procedure on these spy trips is to jot down notes at random during the game as things take my eye. Then, later, I make an analysis of these notes plus other ideas which have come into my mind.

At half time I make notes on the general tactics that the other team employs, the formation that they use, for example. Basically, of course, I don't see the whole game properly. I find that I am concentrating on the one team totally and part of that calls for watching their players position themselves when they are off the ball. It has to be noted where their defenders position themselves when the team is pushing into attack and conversely, where their forwards are when they are being forced into defence. So, you don't spend your time simply watching the action. You have to try to get to know the one team, the team you must beat. I try to get inside the team, try to think the way they might think so you can then assess how they may react to certain situations.

I rated Bayern very highly indeed. Their tactical discipline was excellent and their physical condition was tremendous. They were quite obviously coached to a high degree and some of their inter-passing movements underlined this for me. Really, I felt that they were a far superior team than they had been the last time we met them eighteen months or so earlier. Yet, at the same time, I didn't subscribe to the idea that it would be our toughest game in Europe . . . because as far as I was concerned all the opponents we had faced in Europe had provided us with different problems. Rennes, the French team we had faced in the first round had had a lot of speed on the wings; Sporting Club of Portugal had been very fast and had fantastic skills; Torino had had these same Latin skills plus an unusual aggression for an Italian team. So I wasn't prepared to put any game as more difficult than another. But,

Franz
Beckenbauer

Gerd Muller

nor was I going to under-estimate the West Germans in any way at all. . . .

Still, like all teams, I was convinced that somewhere there would be a weakness that we could play on. Not just a weakness of a single individual but a team weakness we could exploit in the two games we had to play. While I was watching them in action there had been an idea nagging at the back of my mind that I couldn't pin down. It was still there when I sat down in my hotel room later that same night to make my detailed notes on the Bayern team. Then, in the early hours of the morning, it struck me. Suddenly I realised that I had found the weakness I had been looking for.

Bayern were a team with too many *prima donnas*. Not just the big name twosome that all the world knows— Beckenbauer and Muller—but some of the others as well. They showed signs of temper at the odd moment in the game when things didn't go right for them and so I reckoned that if we could pressure them and ruffle them they might be forced into making mistakes and these mistakes could win us the game! They struck me, I suppose, as a team with low morale, a team who would not show too much fighting spirit when things were running against them in a game. Eventually, looking back on the two matches we had with them, I believe that I was proved one hundred per cent right in that assessment.

As we approached the games we made up our minds that we had to pressure them at certain points and from there we had to use our superior speed and strength. I had made individual observations, of course, on the Bayern players and presented that dossier to the players when I returned. In fact, what follows below is the man for man breakdown of the West German team from which we plotted our tactics for the two games, the individual assessments that helped us plan for our victory in the semi-final tie. . . .

Here it is:

MAIER—He looked very confident, came for everything in the air and punched or clutched at exactly the right times. Local reports say that he has been a little bit inactive this year because of a well-organised defence. Kicks a long ball to help set up attacks.

HANSEN—A tall player who attacks whenever he sees that a move upfield is on. He will go all the way to shoot at goal but was not shooting accurately in this game. He has a fair turn of speed but is a slow starter. He marks his man tightly and is good in the air.

65

SCHWARZENBECK—He plays in the centre half position and is a strong, powerfully built player. He does not attack too often, though he will break if an opportunity comes up. Again he is good in the air and marks well. I did not see him tested for pace in this game.

BECKENBAUER—As we know he is a brilliant passer of the ball. But he does not like to make tackles or to be tackled by an opposing player. He is "sweeper" and handles the job superbly on the ground and in the air. I have a strong feeling that he could be pressured into making mistakes because he does not like being challenged.

BREITNER—Another player who likes to attack, though he has no real pace to go down the wings. In spite of that he does a good job of checking out and then getting the ball over into goal where he always seems to be trying to find Muller. Again marks tightly but I think he could be beaten on his left side. Did not look impressive against a dribbler and Hansen was the same. They always held off waiting for cover.

ROTH—Strong and aggressive player. Always looking to do blind side runs which he excels at. He has the pace and the strength to finish these runs, too. Scored a goal from one of them. He did, however, have to take rests during the game before he could come back strongly again.

ZOBEL—He was the man who slotted in to do the midfield covering when any of the defenders went off on attacking runs. He is very accomplished when it comes to playing 1–2 passing movements. He didn't get into the penalty box too much but overall he was a very effective member of the team.

HOENESS—He is a well built young player who seems anxious to work hard at all times. Another player who is good at blind side runs which carry him behind the opposing midfield men. He is always looking for a shot but still defends very well. He checks back strongly and tackles hard.

KRAUTHAUSEN—Tall player who did not really have a go at taking on his full back. He crossed well for Muller's goal in this game. Fair pace, checks back strongly and marks his full back when attacks break down. But I felt that he could have done more work off the ball.

MULLER—He got to every ball he went for in the penalty box. He does all the orthodox setting-up. He lays the ball off brilliantly when being tightly marked and gets into the box as early as possible. Once there he goes for every ball like a tiger. He scored two good goals and had eight or nine shots from difficult positions. He is magnificent in the box and has to be

66

marked tightly. He sets all the attack patterns when Bayern approach goal.

SUHNHOLZ—He is a big, rangy player who didn't do a lot of dribbling runs. Moves around all the time but rarely gets himself into the box. Back checks on his full back very strongly and tackles when he has to. Again good at 1–2 plays.

SCHNEIDER who replaced Hoeness—He got into the game right away when he came on and did a good job in the midfield as well as trying several runs down the wing. Fair pace.

In attack and in defence they always moved as a team. The man who happened to be in possession was always supported and had several alternatives no matter where the ball was. All the players seemed able to do dangerous blind side runs and use wall passes. Also all of them were willing to do a great deal of unselfish running. They were not as physical a team as Torino but I believe they are a better drilled team. And they are much better than when we met them last season. They played with a confidence and assurance which Cologne just couldn't break down.

Well, that was the way I saw them as we started to prepare for the games. In tactical terms I liked their passing movements which had been well worked out, and that same thoroughness was obvious in the number of blind side runs they made which were successful. Zobel, one of their relatively unknown players, did a lot of covering. He impressed me even although his reputation couldn't match so many of the others in the team. He was not an international player and there was little glamour attached to him but he worked hard. It was quite appropriate that he and Alex MacDonald should have been involved in personal duels in the games we played. They just about took each other out of the matches and Alex is for us exactly the kind of player Zobel is for Bayern.

In the first game in Munich we found ourselves under a great deal of pressure in the first half when almost all of them tried to break from defence. But we gave just about as good as we had to take and that is saying something when you are playing away from home in Europe. We deserved to get the equaliser at the start of the second half. Before that we had trailed to a goal scored by Breitner halfway through the first half. Then Colin Stein had hammered a ball across goal, it had gone to Zobel who tried to clear but put it past his own keeper. After that we finished the game stronger than the West Germans. In fact that was part of the pattern of all our games in Europe . . . we always finished up the stronger team. I reckon that to be a tribute to the physical condition we have managed to get the players into. There were a lot of jokes at one time about Rangers training on the sand dunes at Gullane . . . but in these European games I think that the sand dunes' work outs were more than justified. None of the opposing teams could live with us when it came to the closing stages of any of these games. . . .

When the second leg was played at Ibrox against Bayern it was probably the most satisfying match since I took over as the Rangers' coach. The team played brilliantly in the first half. We destroyed Bayern completely and with a little luck would have been leading by four goals at half time instead of the two we got.

There were a lot of close things around their goal that night including a Colin Stein header which hit the bar. The goal that set us on our way came in just forty-five seconds when Sandy Jardine scored. That was a bonus for us, there is no doubt about that. It was the kind of start you only dream about . . . and it came for us on the night we wanted it most. From then on we were in control and stayed in control with young Derek Parlane crashing in a second goal after a corner from Willie Johnston.

Derek had been brought into the team at the last minute as a replacement for our captain John Greig who had been injured. Still only a teenager he came in to play like a veteran. He was handed the job of marking the highly experienced Franz Roth and he did it perfectly. The great thing about the laddie that night was that not only did he mark Roth but he was always ready, too, to break when the chance came. He was well clear of Roth when the chance came for him to score, for instance.

Anyhow the game went the way we wanted it to go from the very beginning. The longer the game went the more the morale of the Bayern team sunk just as I had felt it would do. They began to fight amongst themselves and the normally cool and unworried Beckenbauer looked anxious and flustered as we powered in on him and the rest of his defence. As for little Muller, the most dangerous striker in Europe, I doubt if he has ever had as quiet a match.

In the first half I can only remember a header from him at goal and in the second game he did not manage a single try. Colin Jackson stuck close to him all the time and we also tried to cut off the supply of passes to him. We succeeded better than we had hoped. He finished the game going deeper and

68

deeper trying to get the ball and still not being successful. When you can do that to a player of his standing then there isn't much wrong with you as a team . . .

Mind you, the brilliant attacking football that we hit them with before half time wasn't the only pleasing feature for me in the game. I was happy, too, at the way we played when we were in front. After all it was a tight rope of a game. We couldn't afford to do anything rash. We had to show a bit of caution and that's exactly what the lads did. Earlier in the

Europe's number one striker Gerd Muller of Bayern Munich . . . Wallace wrote in his report that Muller 'must be marked tightly'. It worked and Muller did not score.

season we had almost ruined a great night when we played Sporting Club of Portugal in the same tournament. We had hammered into a 3–0 lead in the first half and then in two careless moments in the second half allowed them in to score twice. That had happened because we had gone looking for more goals when we didn't need to. Against Bayern we knew that the two goals were enough to take us into the final and with the memory of the other game still fresh with us we kept it cool. That proved once more just how much the team had matured in European competition. . . .

Rangers' outside-left Willie Johnston is lectured by the Torino goalkeeper after an incident in their game.

My Double Role with Rangers

by DEREK JOHNSTONE

I suppose there might come a time in my career when I have to make the choice between being a goal getter and a goal stopper . . . and, at the moment I admit to liking the less glamorous role of stopping other people from scoring goals a little better.

That may sound strange from a player whose reputation was made by scoring a goal from the centre forward position when playing for Rangers in the League Cup Final against Celtic. The goal meant Rangers won the game 1–0, won the Cup, and beat their oldest rivals. It also meant that I had become a first team player as a centre forward and the striker's role was what I seemed sure to fill for the rest of my career. At that time in October, 1971, no one—and I include myself in this—would have dreamed that just a little over a year later I would be heading into the first team squad as a defender! Yet that's how my career was turned crazily upside down last season when the Boss (Manager Willie Waddell) decided that I should be given a run at centre half in the reserve team. And so I became a player with a double role at Ibrox, one game playing upfield trying to get the goals to win a game and the next dropping back deep into defence in a bid to stop them.

Of course the coaching staff at Ibrox are all great believers in allowing young players to slot into various positions until they can find their best spot.

This tends to give a young player a real grounding into all the different aspects of the game. Anyhow, I was picked for one of these 'positional experiments' in a reserve game against St Johnstone when I found myself pitched into the defensive job right out of the blue.

Mind you, it wasn't all strange to me because I had played as a centre half when I was at school in Dundee and I had some idea on how to play there. Not long after that I was back in the

71

first team against Ayr United—at CENTRE HALF. And I loved it. To begin with I reckoned that the move to the back was only temporary while the coaching staff worked on giving me as much experience as possible. But, instead, the defensive thing persisted on and off for the rest of the season and is still going on. Mr Waddell has said that he still cannot make up his mind on my best position for the team and he believes that I can adapt to the different challenges thrown up by the two roles I have. It's great to have him talk that way about me . . . and I like the idea of having two strings to my bow so to speak. You know, when you're a striker you might suddenly lose your scoring touch, the way it happens to all goal scorers, and to have another position to drop into is tremendous. I have enjoyed the change enormously because I think that it has not only broadened the scope of my play but it has also helped improve my ball control a lot.

Possibly, too, it has helped make a lot of the fans realise that I can do a little bit more than just head a ball. After that one goal against Celtic at Hampden a lot of folk seemed ready to dismiss me as a kid who could head the ball, get a goal or two and do nothing else. That was Derek Johnstone summed up as far as these fans were concerned. I don't suppose they meant that to be cruel in any way but sometimes I did feel a little bit hurt. Anyhow, that's all over now and I think the fans are accepting me as a little bit more than a one game wonder.

I suppose the game that finally convinced people that the move back to centre half was a good one for me and for Rangers, was the Cup replay with Falkirk. I was brought in to mark Alex Ferguson, the former Rangers' player who always seems determined to do well against us now that he has moved on to another club. I thought that I played well that night and afterwards the Boss gave me the highest praise he had ever given me. He compared me to Willie Woodburn who must have been one of the greatest centre halves that Rangers have ever had. I never saw Woodburn play, of course, and I haven't even seen him on film but the way the older Rangers' fans talk about him he must have been a wonderful player. To be compared to him at Ibrox is something special.

It was after that game that I began to think more and more that maybe the centre half job was going to be the main one given to me . . . and the Cup Winners Cup quarter final against Torino in Italy helped confirm that.

We had decided to use a new defensive formation for that match against the Italians in their own Stadio Communale in

Dave Smith moves into action at Ibrox with all the calmness that
Derek Johnstone says has helped him in his first team run.

Turin. (Davie Smith goes into the plan in detail in another chapter—*Editor*.) I was handed an important marking job, picking up their main striker, an Italian Under 23 international player, Pulici. He was a player the Boss had talked about a lot during his tactics' discussions building up to the match. He had watched Torino play and had come back very impressed by this fellow Pulici. He was a powerful player, dangerous in the box and not afraid of physical contact as some Continentals tend to be. This was the player I was asked to mark in my first competitive game abroad and I must admit that I felt a little bit worried about the task I had been given.

Before the game, though, John Greig and Davie Smith pulled me aside to give me some advice about how I should approach the job. They are the two players in the team with the most European experience and they have helped me considerably. They warned me what I should expect from that game in Turin. They told me that Pulici would try to rough me up a bit, that I could expect a few nasty things to be happening off the ball because that was the way the Italians played in Europe when they were at home. And they both stressed that I must not become involved in any feuding because that was exactly what the Italians wanted you to do.

By trying to make you lose your temper they believe that you can lose your concentration at the same time. That leads to your making mistakes which they might be able to punish. I listened to John and Davie and I took their advice . . . although it wasn't as easy as I thought to stay out of trouble. Pulici behaved exactly as the lads had told me he would behave but I refused to become involved and concentrated on doing the job the Boss had handed to me. The nervousness which I had felt before the game had gone once the match had started. The butterfles I'd felt in the dressing room disappeared once I started playing—as they almost always do—and I think I'm quite lucky in this way, lucky, too, that I have Davie Smith beside me in the defence. You know that if you happen to slip up and make any mistake then Davie is right behind you always ready to cover for errors that are committed. He is always there and he gives everyone else in the defence so much confidence. You feel free to go in tight on the opponent you have been asked to mark because if the ball does get past you then Davie will be there to take care of it. These tactics suited the team, and not only in defence, because in the two games we played this way on the Continent we were able to score valuable away goals, too, in Turin and in Munich.

In both these matches, against Torino and against Bayern Munich, the two front runners we used were Willie Johnston and Colin Stein and the freedom to roam right across the front line seemed to suit both of them. They ran and ran and ran in these games, sometimes without reward but always keeping defenders occupied, forcing them to remain back. In the match against the Italians Willie was able to score a first half goal and in the one against the West Germans Colin took a lot of credit for the move which ended with their inside right Zobel heading past his own goalkeeper.

Tactics when they work as successfully as these did cannot really be criticised. I found that it was great to be able to slot into the team in a different role in the games. For example, in the match at Ibrox against the Italians my role altered slightly once again. Pulici did not play at Ibrox because they had decided to insist on caution. I had been told before the game that if they did not attack as much as they had in Turin then I was to free myself a little from the wholly defensive job. It meant, in fact, that I pushed forward, making one of their players operate from a deeper position and helping us gain the initiative once more. It was a slight change and the experience in that game helped prepare me for the match in Munich where I was able to come out a bit more than I had in Turin. I was marking Uli Hoeness in that game, a young player who had just broken through to the West German international team and who was a key player in their Olympic squad.

I was looking forward to marking Hoeness, mainly because I quite enjoy the challenge that a specific marking job provides. Hoeness makes it difficult for anyone detailed to mark him because he moves around a lot. He doesn't stay in a static position alongside the main striker Gerd Muller. Instead he drops back a little and starts most of his runs from deeper positions. He likes to play a lot of one-two passes, as most of the Germans did. They were particularly good at this, much better at it than the Italians. It's a kind of one touch football where the players move the ball around swiftly and accurately even when in tight positions. It makes it hard to mark anyone when the ball is moving around like that but it added to the challenge as far as I was concerned. I admired the ability of the Bayern team more than any of the other teams we came up against last year. The Italians probably had better individual skills, at least more highly developed skills, but the way the West Germans pushed that ball around was magnificent.

A lot of people, of course, kept wondering how it was that a team like ourselves could do so well in Europe but could fail to be as impressive at home. Well, I have a bit of a theory on that subject. I reckon that the team always played better when we were up against things. I mean, really up against it, facing some of the finest teams in Europe, and knowing when we went out onto the field how important the game was and how big the occasion was and how vital it was to get a result.

All of these things combined put the boys on their toes last season and unfortunately we didn't seem able to stay on the boil for the ordinary league games. It was as if we weren't able to raise the same kind of excitement in ourselves to stay on edge. I know that I didn't have the same edginess on my play in some of the lesser league games as I did in Turin or in Munich. I'm not suggesting that this is the way we should have been . . . all I'm saying is how I felt at times during the season. It is something that we must sort out and all of us know that. We have to stay on edge for all the opposition we are facing, whether it is in a European game with seventy thousand fans or at one of the smaller Scottish grounds with maybe only around ten thousand people there.

Really, no matter how hard the games are, I wouldn't mind facing teams of the quality of Torino and Bayern every week and I'm sure that we would do well against them. Our record in Europe proves that!

It also proved for me that I could hold down my place as a centre half in the first team and I worked hard to perfect my defensive strengths. I try hard when I'm at the back not to give the ball away when I am making clearances. I always try to place any headers to one of the other lads around me and if the ball is on the ground then I'll try to push a short pass to one of my team-mates who are in the clear and this allows them to start the build up to a move.

I always reckon that it's a good thing for me if I can win the ball and then shove a pass to Davie Smith, who always seems to be in the clear and is always looking for the ball, or John Greig and Alex MacDonald who are usually the midfield men. Again these two are always looking for the ball and instead of wild clearances which can put you under pressure very quickly again, you can give them the ball and watch attacking moves start. I get a great deal of satisfaction from this and maybe some of Davie Smith's influence is rubbing off on me. He is a great believer in starting creative moves in defence and I feel the same way about things. I want to win possession . . . and then I want the team to retain possession. I don't want to

give the ball away to the opposition.

This is something that I have been working hard on and another aspect of my game I've been trying to improve is my shouting. I used to be quiet on the field but gradually, after having it hammered into me by the Boss and Jock Wallace and by Davie and John Greig on the field I have started to shout more and more. I find myself, nowadays, shouting at goal-keeper Peter McCloy during a game and that's something I

The defensive role is demonstrated by young Derek Johnstone with this sliding tackle on Hibs' forward Jim O'Rourke in the first of the Scottish Cup semi-final clashes between Rangers and the Easter Road club.

wouldn't have dreamed of doing before. But there are certain situations which demand shouting from defenders and that's why I am getting into the habit . . . even if it does annoy big Peter at times!

The only thing I don't know is when I will settle into one position. That is up to the manager. Another player he has compared me with is John Charles, the great Welsh international who was able to shuttle between the two positions, centre half and centre forward, all through his long career. I'm doing the same just now and I'm happy enough to do what the Boss wants. As long as I can get into the first team and as long as I have the chance of playing in these European games and helping Rangers, then I won't be complaining. Scoring goals or stopping them . . . if it's for Rangers then I don't mind which I do.

Mission In Moscow

As the two Iron Curtain giants of the European Cup Winners Cup tournament of last season, Dynamo Moscow and Dynamo East Berlin, settled their semi-final tie in the Russian city of Llov just twenty-four hours after Rangers had beaten Bayern Munich to qualify for the Barcelona final, Ibrox boss Willie Waddell began his preparations for a spy trip to Russia.

Moscow Dynamo won their semi-final on penalty kicks and Waddell was immediately determined that he MUST see the Russian giants in action. He was insistent that he had to lift the Iron Curtain of secrecy which had shrouded the Moscow team from the time the tournament started. He had been able to watch every other team Rangers had played on their triumphant march through Europe . . . and he felt it essential to his pre-match planning that he see the Russians as well. Mind you, he did have some knowledge of their players and their style. Eighteen months before Dynamo had come to Glasgow to play at Ibrox in a special game to mark the twenty-fifth anniversary of their famous game against Rangers at the close of the Second World War. Rangers had won 1–0 that night through a goal scored by Derek Johnstone.

It meant that Rangers were not going into the game totally blind but Manager Waddell stressed—'Teams change in eighteen months. New players come in and new tactics can be devised and I want an up-to-date picture of what we have to face in the final in Barcelona.'

He did not realise then, however, just how difficult the task of seeing Dynamo in action was to prove. For weeks he bombarded Moscow with messages asking for full details of the Dynamo fixtures . . . for weeks he tried to obtain a visa to visit Russia where he would see Dynamo in action. And for weeks he waited in vain for a reply from Moscow. Then, eventually, the week before the Barcelona game was to be played he

Lev Yashin

achieved the breakthrough that he had wanted. The break-through that he felt he needed. He received confirmation of Moscow Dynamo's home game against another First Division team Kairat, from one of the Eastern regions of the Soviet Union. It was to be played eight days before the Cup Winners Cup final and Waddell was also granted a visa to cover a Moscow stay to see the match. I went with him as the only Scottish journalist able to get a preview of the Russians before the final. We flew out on that Monday morning in a self congratulatory mood. We were happy that things seemed to have slotted into place so perfectly. We could see no further snags. The Soviet Embassy in London had told us that the Sports Committee would look after us on our arrival in the Russian capital. It was, I suppose, too good to be true . . .

And the snags began when we landed at Sheremetievo Airport. There was no one there to meet us. No one seemed to know who the Rangers' manager was or what his mission to Moscow was all about. Eventually in our hotel, standing in the shadow of the Kremlin, we won just a single concession from officials.

The sole privilege we were allowed was that the following day we could go to the Dynamo Stadium and would be allowed to move to the head of the queue to BUY tickets for the match!

When Willie Waddell emphasised once more that he was manager of Rangers and he would require 'special tickets' he was brusquely informed—'You will take whatever tickets they can give you at the stadium.'

And as the rain lashed down on our hotel that night Waddell glumly admitted to me: 'This is the most difficult spy trip I have ever undertaken. You just seem to get nowhere fast. All we can do is hope that something better comes up in the morning. The only consolation I have is that I have got here and I will be able to watch the game somehow.'

But there remained a gloomy feeling that the trip we had started in such good humour was not to be as successful as we had first thought.

Suddenly, though, the next morning the whole atmosphere changed. The problems we had faced on our arrival vanished before wide smiles of welcome and fantastic co-operation from everyone we met. We were taken to the Dynamo Stadium, introduced to the stadium manager and tickets were promptly arranged for that night. Then another meeting was arranged for the next day between Waddell and Dynamo officials.

Back row (left to right)—G. Struthers, A. Conn, G. Fyfe, C. Jackson, G. Neef, P. McCloy, B. Watson, D. Johnstone, G. Donaldson, A. Miller, I. McDonald.

Middle row (left to right)—J. Wallace (Coach), T. Craig (Physiotherapist), C. Stein, N. Pirrie, W. Mathieson, J. Denny, R. McKinnon, G. McCallum, S. Jardine, A. Penman, D. Smith, G. Walker, S. Anderson (Ass. Coach), J. Craven (Trainer).

Front row (left to right)—Willie Waddell (Manager), W. Henderson, B. Semple, A. MacDonald, T. Alexander, J. Greig, D. Parlane, T. McLean, A. Morrison, W. Johnston, Willie Thornton (Ass. Manager).

83

The important thing, however, was the game itself, Dynamo's sixth League game of their new season and it soon became obvious to me that Willie Waddell had been right in maintaining the necessity of his Moscow visit. For there was a surprise for Waddell . . . and a warning to Rangers from that game.

They came from the same source, from the ageing star of the Dynamo team Josef Sabo . . . one time foe of Rangers' Old Firm rivals Celtic in two European clashes with Dynamo Kiev and a former World Cup star with his country. Sabo had joined Moscow Dynamo a year before and although he was now on the wrong side of thirty he was quite clearly the man who made Dynamo click. That night against Kairat, Willie Waddell and I watched a game that could only be described as the Josef Sabo show. Sabo was outstanding. He began the game as 'sweeper' and was magnificent there. He moved into midfield when Dynamo went a goal down and was equally effective there. And eventually he scored the equaliser to give Dynamo a 1–1 draw.

The Moscow fans jeered most of their players from the field—because it was a game they had been expected to win. But for Sabo there were cheers all the way and Waddell had received the warning for his team from a player who had changed Dynamo's tactics from the time eighteen months before when they had played at Ibrox.

Afterwards Waddell told me: 'I had seen quite a few of their players before . . but I had not seen the team with Sabo playing. He makes so much difference and just through his play we will have to revise some of our thoughts about the game in Barcelona.

'Sabo is the thermometer of the team. It is through Sabo that you can judge how things are going. He guides the way the team plays and coaxes some of the less experienced men through a game. Whether it is in defence or in attack everything seems to be controlled by that one man. It was an astonishing performance and it convinced me that he will have to be kept occupied as much as possible in Spain.'

Then the Rangers' boss added: 'The opposition is as difficult as I imagined it would be. No team can ever reach a European final without being a good team, without being a team that you must respect. If Moscow Dynamo were not that kind of team then they would never get close to a final in a European tournament such as this one.

'They looked solid in defence tonight and their wingers,

though they did not do so much in this game, proved to me that on their day they could be the types to win games almost on their own. I wanted to take a look at the wingers because I had heard about them and I am very glad that I was able to see them in this game. Both of them, the outside right Estrokhov and the outside left Evriuzhikin have been in the Russian national team and have been successful at that level. That is enough to make us realise their potential danger . . . .

'Another aspect of their play which I noted was that their full backs Basalaev and Dolmatov were always ready to come forward into attack. This will be as difficult a task for us as the semi final games against Bayern Munich were.'

The next day at a convivial meeting with the Russian officials, the greatest Soviet soccer star of all time, the goal-keeping giant Lev Yashin, now technical director of Dynamo, talked freely about his team and about Rangers. Yashin, much more forthcoming than most Russians, confirmed Waddell's view that Sabo was the guiding genius behind Dynamo's European success run, and the man who influenced the younger players in the Moscow side. Smiling he told me: 'Sabo has been the inspiration of Dynamo this season. He has a deep knowledge of the game and his experience in so many European games at club level and top international games, too, has helped us immeasurably this season. Sabo is one of these rare players who never loses form. There are no highs or lows in his performances for the team. He is always himself. He is always Sabo and that means he is always a great, great player for our club.

'And yet we are not a one man team. Certainly Sabo is a man we rely on to provide inspiration for the others and, perhaps, in Barcelona, his experience will be needed to calm the nerves of our other players who have not taken part in so many important games. They will be nervous and we know that . . . because they are the first Soviet club team to play in a European tournament final.'

It was that closing remark which emphasised in my mind once more the immensity of the task which faced Rangers in Barcelona the following week. In that stadium office littered with trophies and pennants from clubs and tournaments across the world, the huge question of Soviet sports' prestige had been raised . . . and it was clear from the officials present that this was of immense importance to them. A moment later Yashin underlined just how important it was to the Soviet authorities when he said: 'If our players can win the European

Cup Winners Cup then they will have performed a tremend-ous service for Soviet football and will almost certainly be made Masters of Sport. It is the greatest honour that any athlete can receive in the Soviet Union and only a few footbal-lers have earned it. I have been honoured as have Shesternev and Metreveli, two of our great international players. Now we believe that all the Dynamo players will join us in that list of honour.'

The title Master of Sport means more to any Russian than even the huge bonuses paid by clubs such as Inter Milan mean to Italian players. It is an award which is treasured by everyone in the Soviet Union . . . and these Dynamo players wanted desperately to win it. That did not bode well for Rangers as they prepared for the game in Barcelona.

There were other things, too, building up against the Scots. At one time the club sides from Russia had refused to enter for the European club tournaments because vital ties had to be played during their break from football in mid-winter.

Although adjustments have been made to dates in a bid to help the Eastern European nations a problem still remains. The quarter final ties generally have to be played hard on the heels of that winter shut-down and the teams have to face that hurdle without proper preparation. This time, though, the Russians had met another team from the East, Red Star of Belgrade at that stage and then in the semi-finals, yet another Iron Curtain team in Dynamo East Berlin. Now they were going into the final as their season OPENED. They were going into the final with players fresh and eager after just six league matches. Rangers, on the other hand, were heading for Bar-celona at the end of an arduous season. And then, too, the Scots had had to arrange two warm-up games in a bid to keep in trim. While Rangers had to trek to the Highlands to play a game against an Inverness Select and then play another game against Second Division St Mirren at Love Street . . . the Rus-sians were playing ordinary League games with the freshness which accompanies every team at the start of a new season.

This was a worry to Rangers and while Lev Yashin dropped into the well-worn routine of all Continental coaches of play-ing down his team's form and achievements I knew that Ran-gers had problems to overcome. Yashin kept emphasising how well Rangers had done in Europe. He kept telling us how many fine teams they had defeated on the road to Barcelona and how the Dynamo opposition had not been nearly so good. On the face of things Yashin was speaking honestly. . . .

Yashin insisted—'To beat Sporting Club of Portugal and then Torino and finally Bayern Munich—these are achievements that any team in the world would be proud to have accomplished. We had it so very much easier. In the first round we beat Olympiakos Piraeus of Greece and then Eskisehirspor of Turkey in the next round. Only in the quarter final did we beat a team who could be compared with any of the sides that the Rangers had to defeat on their way to the final. Red Star of Belgrade had a formidable record and many fine players and it was our best display in the competition to beat them. Rangers have had many great performances . . . we have had just that one.'

Waddell listened politely but refused to be taken in by Yashin's stream of compliments for his team and their achievements. He knew only too well that he had his own problems to deal with . . . and he knew, also, that the biggest problem of all would be Josef Sabo. If Sabo could not be curbed then Rangers would not win the European trophy they had hunted for so long.

Seeing Sabo in action and judging his influence on the team had made Waddell's mission to Moscow worth while. And on the long journey home as Waddell studied his notes the name Sabo leapt out time and again to emphasise that Dynamo's ageing star would be the barrier between Rangers and the European Cup Winners Cup.

Playing The Italian Game

by DAVE SMITH

The Italians have a word for it, one of the most hated words in football's international vocabulary . . . they call it catenaccio.

And in soccer terms it means one of the tightest possible defensive formations that any side can use. It originated in Italy where its high priest was the famous coach of Inter Milan Helenio Herrera. He brought this defensive formation to near perfection and for several years ruled both Italy and Europe as he employed this strategy. But at the same time as he brought success to his club he helped spoil the game as a spectacle for Italian fans as every other club gradually adopted his rigid policies.

Yet it was the very same system that Rangers slotted into when we went to Turin for the first leg of the quarter final tie in the European Cup Winners Cup last season! It was a shock to the Italians as well as to our own fans who had travelled to Italy to support us in the game. But it was a tremendous success in that first match and that was what mattered most of all to us.

But, really, if you examined the situation the Rangers' fans who travelled to Turin should not have been too surprised at the choice of tactics for the game. After all, the Boss (Manager Willie Waddell) had once gone to study Inter Milan's methods and Herrera's tactics when he was manager of Kilmarnock. Almost ten years after that trip to see Herrera the lessons paid off when we travelled to Italy to face one of their leading teams.

The basic formation was reasonably simple. As the usual 'sweeper' in the side my position had been alongside the orthodox centre half Colin Jackson. I played around his position but this new system called for me taking a step back to play behind Colin while young Derek Johnstone was brought in to play beside him. This meant really the team were playing

Rangers' 'sweeper' Dave Smith who explains the tactics used by the Ibrox club against Torino in the European Cup Winners Cup quarter final.

Rangers wing half Dave Smith (left) and Dundee United's inside forward Archie Knox go for this ball.

Rangers wing half Dave Smith beats United player Archie Knox (right) to this ball to score Rangers only goal.

**Rangers wing half Dave Smith beats United players Archie Knox
and keeper Hamish McAlpine (right) to score Rangers only goal.** 91

Rangers wing half Dave Smith raises his arm in the air after he
had scored the winning goal against Dundee United.

two centre halves with myself as an additional defender at the back of them. Colin and Derek were given the job of handling the two main Torino strikers, Bui and Pulici while I stayed at the back to plug any gaps that might appear and gather any through balls which might elude the other two.

Then, in midfield, we had Tommy McLean, John Greig and Alex MacDonald with just two players, Willie Johnston and Colin Stein doing all the front running. It was a system that the Boss had devised to frustrate the Italians because he reckoned, after watching them, that they would throw everything at us while playing at home. In the pre match talks

Dave Smith in action against his old team, Aberdeen, as he slides in to rob ex-Ranger Jim Forrest as the Dons' forward moves in on goal.

he had emphasised that unlike the majority of Italian teams Torino would push into attack without showing to much caution. So in practice games before we left Scotland our new set up was tried out until we had settled into the system. When we reached Turin we knew that the Boss had been right. For the Torino coach Gustavo Giagnoni was young and ambitious and according to everyone we met he scorned the defensive ploys of the other coaches, insisting that his team play attacking football.

What Giagnoni didn't realise, however, was that he would come up against a defensive style when he met us. He had come to watch us and we had played in our normal way, with no hint of our intentions for the game in Italy. He must have expected us to come out and play the open football we use in Scotland. He was not prepared for the new-look Rangers he found that night in the Stadio Communale. Basically he did not believe that a Scottish team would be able to show enough tactical discipline to play such a rigidly applied game. But the set-up suited us. The two main strikers were marked very closely by Colin and Derek while I picked up anyone who got past then. After the game Giagnoni told Italian pressmen—'Rangers came here and played the Italian game. It was too defensive but it is the kind of game that Italian teams have used often when they are away from home in a European tie and we can have no complaints.'

He was right, of course, it was the Italian game, the style of play which had frustrated so many teams in other countries and now we had turned the tables on them. In a way it was quite ironic that we should do this in of all places Italy, the home of catenaccio! Mind you there were times in that game, especially a spell at the start of the second half, that we were put under fantastic and unrelenting pressure from the desperate Torino team.

Of course, when you play any top team away from home in a European tie then you expect to be placed under severe pressure. The other team tends to have more of the ball and you are forced to lie back a little, hoping to keep them out and, if you get lucky, grab a goal which can help you when the second leg is played on your ground.

I've faced pressure in a lot of countries, now. In Yugoslavia against Vojvodina Novi Sad. In West Germany against Borussia Dortmund. In Spain against Real Saragossa. Eventually you learn to live with the pressure because it is part of these games in Europe. But that night in Turin I faced an

onslaught quite unlike any I had had to face in the past. Once, in that game against Borussia Dortmund, who were holders of the Cup Winners Cup at the time, we were in trouble. We had gone there knowing that to lose a single goal could put us out of the tournament and we fought to get a 0–0 draw against a team which included two of the West German players who were in the 1966 Cup Final, Sigi Held and Lothar Emmerich. Until Italy last season that night in Dortmund had been the worst pounding we had taken . . . Turin beat it. They attacked at the start of the second half in a way I did not think any Italian team could attack. The previous night in the same giant stadium we had seen their great local rivals Juventus play Wolves in the European Union Cup. They had drawn with the English side and shown a remarkable lack of drive for a team playing on their own ground. All out attack just didn't seem to be considered but while they showed that Italian trait of caution Torino were so different. . . .

Luckily we had the Boss's warning to prepare us and his perfectly planned tactics to help us when our game got under way. He had spotted the danger men and had also seen

Dave Smith accepts his award as the Scottish Football Writers' Association Player of the Year from the Leader of the Opposition Mr Harold Wilson at the Association dinner in Glasgow.

weaknesses that we might be able to exploit. Bui and Pulici were being kept quiet, John Greig was marking the highly priced international midfield man Claudio Sala and up front Willie Johnston and Colin Stein were keeping their defenders occupied. In fact Willie was able to snatch a first half goal after a wonderful Willie Mathieson overlap had exposed the Italian defence. It sent us into the lead and spurred the Italians to superhuman efforts as they tried to equalise.

When the second half began they came at us like no other team had ever done. Every single one of their players seemed determined to push forward into attack. Sala was shoved forward to join up with the main two strikers; they took off a defender Fosati and replaced him with their international left winger Giovanni Toschi to allow them to vary their attacks. We held out through the worst of these raids and then crumbled just once before them. Just that once we slipped up and when Toschi shot for goal Pulici somehow managed to get a toe to the ball and deflect it past Peter McCloy into the net to level the scores. That goal arrived in sixty four minutes, just nineteen minutes after the start of the second half. . .

It seemed to all of us in the defence, mind you, as if the game had been going on for ever. It was the longest second half that I can ever remember because we were under such constant pressure. Somehow, though, we held out until the end with the scores level at 1–1 and in the closing stages it was the Italians who tired. I suppose that was partly because of the extra effort they had put in . . . but it was also because of our superior fitness. I found in all the games that we played in Europe last season that we finished the stronger team.

The Italians realised this and so during the second half as their frustration increased and their strength drained away they became quite rough. An awful lot of things were happening off the ball. Players were being punched and elbowed with the ball nowhere near them and time after time Pulici tried to involve young Derek Johnstone in trouble on the field. Fortunately the youngster refused to get involved in any feuding . . . he just calmly got on with the game.

When we flew home the following day to Glasgow we realised that the victory we wanted was within our grasps . . . but we realised, too, that the tie was not over. We remembered a lesson from our old Glasgow rivals Celtic who had returned to Scotland two years before after gaining a 0–0 draw with AC Milan in the San Siro Stadium in the European Cup quarter final. Everyone in Scotland thought that the magnificent

An action picture of Rangers' wing-half Dave Smith, Scotland's Player of the Year.

result in Italy meant victory for Celtic . . . everyone felt that the second leg at Celtic Park was nothing more than a formality.

Then came the game and Celtic lost by one goal and were knocked out of that year's European Cup competition. It was a warning to us not to become complacent.

Still, the 1–1 draw had put the pressure on the Italians. For it meant that because of the rule which has away goals counting double in the event of a draw, we could draw 0–0 at Ibrox and still get through to the semi-finals. But for our own fans' sake we wanted to win the game outright.

However, caution was still necessary, and the Boss decided on more or less the same tactics for Ibrox as we had used in the Stadio Communale. The formation was the same but with more freedom for players to break out of defence into attack. On the night we found that Torino wanted to play it carefully even though they were losing—technically at least—from the first leg score! Their idea seemed to be to try to draw us out of position and then strike for the goals they needed so badly. They wanted to lure us upfield and then take advantage of gaps we might leave. They didn't find many. It took them thirty-two minutes to get a shot at goal and it was a long range try which Peter McCloy dealt with easily. Then four minutes before half time they had their most dangerous moment of the match when Toschi hit the post with a shot. That warning proved to us that our cautious approach had been justified. We had found it hard to break down their defence . . . much harder than we had in Turin.

But, while their defence was more organised, their forwards rarely showed the same aggression as they had done in Italy. In fact young Derek Johnstone was able to force his way forward into the midfield and even get up into their box for some very dangerous headers at goal.

Eventually fifty-five seconds after the start of the second half we got the goal we needed to clinch the game, to keep our one hundred per cent European record at Ibrox . . . and to give our fans the victory they wanted to see. Little Tommy McLean picked the ball up in his own half and raced away from the Italian left back Fosati. He left the poor Italian defender trailing and then crossed beautifully into goal. Willie Johnston went up for the ball with their goalkeeper Castellini at the near post . . . but most missed it. And then there was Alex MacDonald running in at the other post to force the ball over the net with his body.. It wasn't the most glamorous ending to a great move . . . but it counted just as

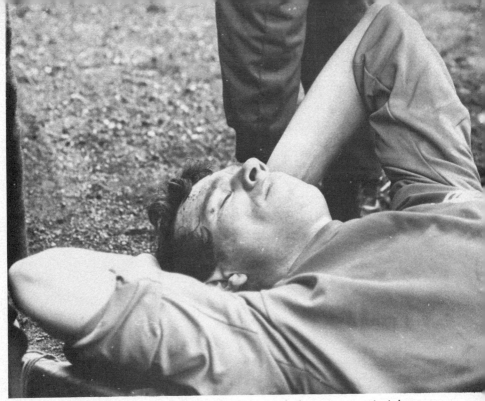
Rangers wing-half Dave Smith is carried away on a stretcher after breaking his leg.

much as any other spectacular goal would have counted. That was all that mattered to us at that moment.

We came close to scoring more goals. Willie Johnston hit the post and Derek Johnstone saw a header booted desperately off the line by the Torino defender, Crivelli. But it was Alex MacDonald's goal which killed the faint hopes that the Italians had had of pulling off a shock result on our ground.

The goal, of course, also carried us through to the semi-finals and brought fresh hope to the seventy-five thousand fans on the Ibrox terracings that night that we might, at long last, bring a European trophy back for them to cheer.

We had not had it easy in any of the three ties we had played. At the opening round of the tournament while we were struggling in the League at home after a disastrous start we had had to face Rennes, then lying in second spot in the French First Division. The next round we had come up against Sporting Club of Portugal, another star-studded combination. Then it had been Torino, powerful challengers for the hard-to-win Italian title.

And so a few days later when the draw for the semi-finals

was made it did not surprise any of us very greatly when we were paired with our old rivals from West Germany, Bayern Munich, who were at the top of their league! Every round seemed to be getting more difficult . . . every game seemed to call for another extra effort . . . every opposing team seemed to be stronger than the last. For Bayern were the toughest team remaining in the tournament. I think, deep down, that all of us had felt that if we were to win the European Cup Winners Cup then at some stage Bayern were the team we would have to beat.

We had lost to them twice before in European competitions. In 1967 they beat us in the Cup Winners Cup Final and the season before last they beat us in the first round of the Fairs Cities Cup. This time, though with our new tactics and our great adaptability we felt that we could turn the tables and get a bit of revenge. The tactics for Turin had been perfect. They had brought a new dimension to our play and we reckoned that we could surprise Bayern . . .

After Torino we did not feel the need to fear anyone. Bayern would be given respect. But we were not afraid of anyone in Europe.

Countdown In Castelldefells

On Sunday morning, May 21, Rangers flew out from Prestwick Airport near Glasgow to prepare for the most important game of the club's long and distinguished history. They settled into a hotel in the small holiday resort of Castelldefells which lay around fifteen miles outside the city of Barcelona where the final of the European Cup Winners Cup was to be played. Their hotel, the Gran Hotel Rey Don Jaime was placed on a hilltop about half a mile from the main coastal road. Its situation ensured the privacy and seclusion that Manager Willie Waddell insists upon for his players before any important European cup clash. . . .

A few hours after the Rangers' arrival Moscow Dynamo flew in on an Air France flight from Paris, the city they had been forced to visit to obtain visas to enter Spain. They had booked themselves into a hotel in the centre of the resort, one that was built on the beach. There was little privacy and no seclusion and the reason for that was that the Russians had not made as thorough advance preparations for the visit to Barcelona as Rangers' Manager Willie Waddell had done.

The following is a description of the build-up to the game, split into a day-by-day account of the happenings around the tiny resort town of Castelldefells which for four days in May became the centre of European football.

SUNDAY—As Rangers emerged from their British Caledonian charter jet with the air hostesses appropriately dressed in tartan uniforms they were greeted by cheers from the first wave of red, white and blue clad fans who had 'follow, followed' ahead of their heroes. As they stepped into the brilliant sunshine the Rangers' players gave an impression of relaxed confidence but to those of us who had travelled with them often in the past there was an edginess apparent and there were troubles lingering around the party for Manager Willie Waddell.

It was in the afternoon around the hotel swimming pool at a press conference that Waddell brought the problems into the open. Skipper John Greig had damaged his ankle again in training at Ibrox towards the end of the previous week. Originally the powerhouse skipper had had no reaction from his comeback work-outs against the Inverness Select and then against St. Mirren. The latest blow had arrived in a training kick-about at the Stadium when he went over on his ankle. Centre-half Colin Jackson, injured at the end of the season, had missed both warm-up games and was doubtful along with Greig. But Waddell declared that both would be considered . . . although no risks would be taken when the final choice was made. He kept little back at the conference. . . .

The players did not train. They spent the day relaxing around the hotel grounds . . . but sun bathing had been quickly banned by Waddell because of the risks.

And so they sat at the pool wearing their royal blue track suits. It was typical of Waddell's eye to thoroughness that the sunbathing ban had come so swiftly. He did not want a single one of the players to be burned before the game in case there were ill-effects which could rule them out. He had brought some food, too, in case there were problems at the hotel.

The Russians were given a magnificent welcome from the Spanish fans at the airport, mainly because of the presence of the smiling Lev Yashin. The legendary goalkeeper was clearly being used as a goodwill ambassador on their arrival. While most of the others maintained the grim, unsmiling outlook that usually characterises Russian football teams Yashin was glad-handing his way around the airport. It was very necessary for Yashin to do this . . . because no-one else made the effort and there were no Russian supporters flying in!

Yashin apart, the Russians remained morosely silent, sheltering behind a bland interpreter who refused to put any questions which he did not approve of. Getting information was next to impossible!

MONDAY—The first training sessions were held by both teams with the ground of Espanol, the number two team in the city of Barcelona, being used. Rangers trained first and then later in the day the Russians took over. The Spanish authorities were being scrupulously fair. Any use of the Barcelona Stadium, the one which was to be used for the

101

The relaxing atmosphere of the Rangers' hotel is shown here as (left to right), Tommy McLean, Alex MacDonald, John Greig, Willie Johnston and reserve goalkeeper Bobby Watson sit around the swimming pool.

The closest the Rangers' players were allowed to swimming in the hotel pool before the game. The three with their feet dangling in the water are left to right, Colin Stein, Alex MacDonald and Gerry Neef with skipper John Greig standing behind them. The sun bathing ban was being strictly enforced as you can see from the track suited players in the sunshine. . . .

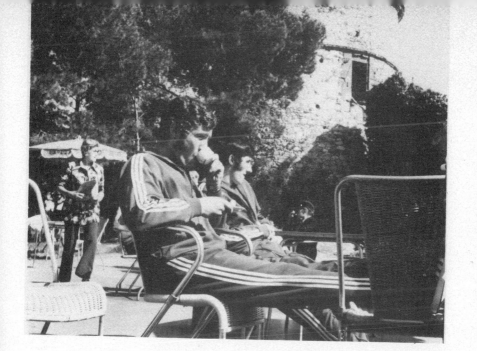

game, had been banned until Tuesday. The reason for this was that the European Union Youth Tournament final was being played there.

In spite of the hordes of Scottish fans flooding into the city of Barcelona and the resorts which are scattered along the Costa Brava there were no invasions of the Rangers' hotel. The peace and quiet that the players had wanted remained undisturbed. Things were vastly different, though, at the Russian HQ down in the town of Castelldefells itself. Monday was a public holiday and the people of Barcelona flocked to the coast. In the town discotheques blared out their music, car horns blasted incessantly and holidaymakers swept into the terraces of the Russian hotel as the players tried to rest. It was an impossible situation and Yashin, his hands over his ears, complained to me: 'If this game was in the Soviet Union then we would have been in a special training camp well away from noises like this. It is not good for our players and if we had known how bad this would be then we would not have stayed here.'

It did not help to tell him that Rangers were able to relax. . . .

There seemed to be a strict regimentation of the Russian side. The players trooped into the dining-room together and left together, speaking to no-one. There appeared to be a rigid time-table and it was one which could not be broken.

Sandy Jardine tries a cup of Spanish tea with reserve Jim Denny in the background . . . in the seclusion of their pre-match HQ.

TUESDAY—Twenty-four hours were left and the final plans were being laid at the rival hotels. Both teams were given their first chance to train on the Barcelona Stadium and the Rangers' players were happy. It was not bare and dry the way so many Spanish pitches can be. The ground was good with a lot of grass and the only problem seemed to be with the atmosphere.

Whether it was because of the heat or because of the construction of the stadium the ball seemed to move strangely in the air for some of the players. They had difficulty in judging their jumps to head the ball.

There were bigger problems, though, for Manager Waddell to face up to. Colin Jackson had a final breakdown in training. He moved in to make a tackle on Tommy McLean and then tried to check himself to avoid crashing into the tiny winger. He succeeded in missing McLean but aggravated an old injury and had to be ruled out. It was a heart-breaking moment for the man who had so successfully shackled Europe's number one goal getter Gerd Muller in the semi-finals.

But on the credit side John Greig was passed fit by the manager and then Willie Waddell announced that he was left with one doubt only . . . and that three players were in the running for one midfield position. The trio who were chasing the place were Andy Penman, Alfie Conn and Derek Parlane. Everyone was trying to work out which player would come in but Manager Waddell parried every question. He refused to be drawn.

Down in the resort the Russians had withdrawn completely from contacts with outsiders . . . particularly Scottish journalists!

There was no talk of a team although it was obvious now that their injured centre-forward Vladimir Koslov would not play. The coach Konstantin Beskov, a former player with the Dynamo club and an opponent of Rangers' boss Willie Waddell in that epic 1945 clash, had imposed an iron discipline on his players. I made an attempt to interview their star Sabo after receiving permission from the club president to do so. Sabo was willing, even the obstructive interpreter was willing, but within a few minutes the interview was over. In a stormy scene in the foyer of the hotel Beskov butted in and ordered Sabo to bed. Tension seemed to have caught up with the Dynamo boss. . . .

WEDNESDAY—This was the day everyone had waited for. It was the season's climax for the Rangers' players and they tried to relax around the hotel without thinking too much about what was to come at night. The journalists were still talking about the midfield problem position and all of us tried to guess who would come in to join Alex MacDonald and John Greig. The general opinion favoured veteran Andy Penman, but as the bus left for the game with the players the news came that Alfie Conn had been chosen. The Russians, predictably, delayed their team until the kick off. . . .

THURSDAY—A champagne celebration ended in the hotel in the early hours of the morning. The Torino coach, Gustavo Giagnoni, had come to congratulate Rangers and finished staying, singing Scots' songs with Ibrox captain John Greig.

There were other friends, too, to wish Rangers well. Swedish promoter Borje Lantzke appeared and outlined plans for a round-the-world tour for the Ibrox team. Toronto soccer impresario Steve Stavro and his right-hand man, Canada's international team boss John McMahon have arrived on a special trans-Atlantic charter to cheer on Rangers and bid to take them to Canada. The world wants Rangers . . . that was obvious.

At lunch-time the team bus left the hotel and headed for the airport. The players were taken direct to the jet on the tarmac to save them from the thousands of fans. But even as we were about to board the plane a group of Scots, also embarking, raced across the tarmac to mob John Greig as he carried the European Cup Winners Cup into the plane. It was an emotional moment as the little resort of Castelldefells dropped from the world of football's gaze after four days of glory as soccer's European capital.

Into Europe With The Babes

It didn't come as much of a surprise to most of the vast Rangers' support to find that the Ibrox babes were thrust into two European tournaments last season to share the Continental limelight with their more distinguished first team colleagues towards the end of last season. . . .

And the reason there were little signs of surprise at the globe-trotting adventures of the youngsters was because all along Manager Willie Waddell has stressed the importance of building a powerful squad of young players as he plans for Rangers' future.

And in these times senior players at all levels must pick up as much Continental experience as possible to develop along the lines expected by the top clubs of today. More and more youth tournaments are being organised each year on the continent . . . and more and more of our top teams are sending their babes to take part in them. They have become sophisticated soccer nurseries . . . almost universities for the completion of the football education of the young players. Not so long ago their education was undertaken in reserve team football at home after a spell in the juniors. Now it is polished on the same European fields that their senior counterparts so often have to play on. Two years ago Rangers broke their duck when they sent a young team to play in a tournament organised by the Dutch Side Ajax in Amsterdam.

Towards the end of last season came a double follow-up . . . a glamour tournament in Portugal organised, once more, by one of Europe's great clubs, Benfica of Lisbon. Then a smaller competition in Holland set up by a Dutch First Division team Go Ahead of Deventer.

The important one was the one in Portugal because it gave the youngsters a real chance to soak up the Continental atmosphere they had been hearing about second hand from the first

George Donaldson, the midfield man in the Rangers' youth team who was carried off in the rough-house match with Red Star, Belgrade in the Lisbon tournament.

team men for the whole of the season. It also gave youth team coach Stan Anderson his first taste of competitive football on the Continent, as a coach or as a player. Anderson made the trip as right hand man to assistant manager Willie Thornton and afterwards he explained: 'I had been over to Rhodesia with Clyde on a tour but that was the limit of my experience abroad so, in a way, I was learning along with the young lads. It was so different from that Rhodesian tour because there were no friendlies involved in this . . . we were learning first hand just how competitive European football can be!

'And we found that out at youth level . . . because, make no mistake, this was simply one of the big European tournaments in miniature. The games had all the aspects that the top level games can throw up including a bit of a dust-up in one of our matches. The whole experience was invaluable for every player we took on the trip. There is nothing at all we could have done at Ibrox which would have given as much to the lads as the trip to Portugal did.'

The eight club tournament had four clubs from the Portuguese First Division, the hosts, Benfica along with Porto, Vitoria Setubal and Academica. The other four clubs taking part were Rangers, Ajax of Holland, Red Star, Belgrade of Yugoslavia and Cagliari of Italy. Unhappily the Rangers' babes were able to win only one of their games . . . but they still returned to Scotland with the trophy which was presented to the team which had played the most attractive football of the competition. It was a trophy they prized as they flew home.

But, let Anderson take up the story of the tournament—

'The competition was limited to players who were under the age of twenty but, of course, we had three of our lads who would normally have qualified to take part, still back at home with the first team. They weren't able to travel with us and going into that kind of company without Alfie Conn, Derek Johnstone and Derek Parlane was just a bit too much of a handicap for us. They would have added a lot of experience—plus skill— to the squad.

'Still, we went to Portugal to get the lads used to playing against different teams in different conditions and, although we would have liked to win, the results this time were secondary. It was the experience we were after and we succeeded in getting that.

'We had to go into some games against teams whose average age was much greater than that of our lads. You see, we took along a fair number of our 'S' form signings, some of them

Centre-half Gus McCallum leads the way over the hurdles in a training session at the Albion. This type of preparation helped him win the Eusebio Trophy in the Benfica tournament in Portugal.

just kids of fifteen or sixteen and at times it looked as if the challenge would be too much for them.

'Anyhow, in the first game nothing seemed too much for them. We played our best football of the tournament and hammered in five goals against Porto to win our opener 5–2. It was a great result, a great boost to the lads ... but it turned out to be a bad thing for us in the long run. For that five goal performance put every other team in the tournament on their guard against us. We played brilliantly in that game and the five goals we scored gave the competition its biggest score. The sad thing for us was that we didn't score another goal in our remaining games.

'These five goals had us marked down as the danger men of the tournament, in spite of having the youngest team of any of the eight clubs taking part. We found that out in our very next game when we were drawn to play against the Yugoslavs, Red Star of Belgrade. From the start I knew we were going to be up against it. Their players were older, bigger and stronger and

Stan Anderson (on left) at the Ibrox tactics' board with coach Jock Wallace. Anderson learned along with the Ibrox babes on the trip to Portugal for the Benfica youth competition.

very much more experienced than us. In fact, four of the team had been playing fairly regularly for their club's First Division side.

'They were 2–0 up at half time and in that first half one of their players had been ordered off and our own George Donaldson had been carried off injured. It was a rough, tough game with the Slavs showing all the same temperamental traits as their elders. We had a lot more of the ball than they did after half time but their keeper was magnificent. He defied us. I felt that if we had been able to get one goal then others would have followed . . . but that first goal eluded us. And so we lost that game and the Slavs went on to win the tournament.

'In our next match we played another of the Portuguese teams, Academica and met up with an old friend of Rangers . . . Fernando Vaz, the man who had been coach of Sporting Club of Portugal when Rangers beat them in the second round of the European Cup Winners Cup. He had lost his job with Sporting Club after that European defeat and he was now in the process of taking over as coach of Academica . . . just as we were facing up to their youth team. We lost this game, too, by 1–0 this time and again just couldn't score a goal though we did play well enough. I was wishing at this stage that we had had Derek Parlane with us or Derek Johnstone because both of them had been scoring goals for the reserves during the season. Afterwards Fernando Vaz told us that Rangers had been the more skilful team and that was kind of him but it did not help us get the goals we wanted.

'We were beginning to wish by now that we had saved some of our five goals from the opening game for the rest of the tournament matches. Because now we were in a goal famine . . . one which continued into the last game we played, and the best game, too, against the Dutch side Ajax of Amsterdam. Again we couldn't score a single goal but, although we lost 1–0 again it was a cracking game. There was great football from the Dutch boys and from us and I think this was the game which clinched the prize for the most attractive team in the competition for us.

'Another trophy we won, of course, was an individual award for the best foreign player who took part in the competition. It was called the Eusebio Trophy and it had been gifted by the great Benfica and Portugal star. Our centre half Gus McCallum was the player who won it. These two prizes which were handed over at the closing banquet helped ease some of the disappointment which a few of the youngsters felt because they had not done better in the tournament as a whole.

'Looking back, though, there was no need for any of them to feel disappointed. We had come to the tournament mainly to gain experience of playing conditions abroad and we had done that. It is invaluable for young players to pick up on things like this at the earliest possible stage in their careers. Older players weren't able to get that experience until they made the first team.

'Already our young players realise the different attitudes and approaches to the game of players from Portugal, from Yugoslavia and from Holland. They know that just from playing in this one tournament. They know, for example, that the Dutch are fairly close to us in their approach, that the Portuguese are highly skilled and can shield the ball with the mastery the Latin races seem to have for this aspect of the game and that the Slavs are highly-strung and temperamentally explosive. It was all a part of their soccer education.'

The youngsters also learned, of course, how to cope with hard, fast grounds . . . how they must be especially careful with their diet when they are in a foreign country . . . how some players can be upset by air travel while others are not . . . and how violence can often erupt in games where different football cultures clash. All of these lessons, simple though they may appear, are important to every young player as he develops. And all of them have to be learned carefully if the youngsters are going to be ready to step into the first team squad when their opportunities come.

It was also an undreamed-of opportunity for some of the younger players who went out with the others. Some of them, Ian Thomson, Billy McNicoll, Davie Scott and Ally Love, for example, are still around the fifteen or sixteen years of age mark . . . and there they were setting off on a football apprenticeship which was surrounded with glamour.

Remember, the youngsters played on magnificent stadiums in front of crowds approaching ten thousand—the tournament opener between Benfica and Ajax actually drew almost thirty thousand fans—and stayed in the best hotels in Portugal.

As well as all these benefits on and off the field assistant manager Willie Thornton and coach Stan Anderson returned to Ibrox with dossiers on all their opponents. As Anderson quickly points out when he talks of the trip: 'A great many of the youth teams follow the same playing pattern of the club sides they represent. We watched them carefully and if the first team comes up against any of the teams we met then we will be able to provide guide lines for the Boss (Manager Willie Waddell).

'Anyhow, in a year or so quite a number of these Red Star of Belgrade players will be in the first team. Four of them have broken through already and some of the others will too. We have a working knowledge of them all from our game and so we have a run down available of them if the first team has to face them in Europe at any time. There is really nothing but good coming out of these trips.'

Nothing appears to be wasted by the Ibrox back room boys. Every scrap of information is noted and later digested and then will be put to use when the opportunity comes up.

But for the kids themselves, for these soccer babes who are starting to learn their chosen trade, the experience is the great thing. They are being tempered for the special demands of European football at an early age. That must pay off in the years to come as Willie Waddell so obviously realises.

In fact, just a few weeks after that Lisbon tournament, the signs of a pay off were already evident. The young Rangers' squad headed for Deventer in Holland to take part in another youth tournament. In five games they lost just once to the English side, Preston North End who won the competition against opposition from the Dutch First Division hosts, Go Ahead, Deventer, Dinamo Zagreb of Yugoslavia, Brugge of Belgium and Drumchapel Amateurs from Scotland.

The best moment came with a revenge for the Red Star, Belgrade troubles in Portugal . . . a 4–0 win over Dinamo Zagreb! And in one of the matches coach Stan Anderson pushed in four of his fifteen year old youngsters . . . and they won.

The future seems bright. . . .

The English Give a Guide to Europe

The annual pre-season clashes with English First Division opposition had brought little success to Rangers over recent seasons . . . but last year changed all that with a vengeance.

Yet when Rangers returned to Glasgow after the disappointment of failing to win the Gothenburg tournament in Sweden their fans were none too confident about the outcome of the games that Manager Willie Waddell had arranged for his players.

When it was announced that the Ibrox team would go into the first match against Everton without centre-forward Colin Stein and outside-right Willie Henderson, who were both injured abroad, the confidence of the fans was scarcely helped. After all, the highly talented Everton team packed with stars such as Keith Newton, Gordon West, Howard Kendall, Colin Harvey, Brian Labone, Alan Ball and Joe Royle, had come north determined to win. Their manager Harry Catterick, an old friend of Rangers' boss Waddell, had laid it on the line when he told me: 'This is not just a friendly as far as either of the teams are concerned and we are well aware of that. This is a game where not only club prestige is at stake . . . the whole question of national pride is the issue when our clubs meet up!'

With Catterick saying that publicly and the Rangers' players knowing that Everton captain Alan Ball would be taking the same line—he always does when he comes up against a Scots' team—it was obvious that this was going to be a real test for Waddell's men.

And yet, as was to happen in all the big occasion games last season, fifty thousand fans saw Rangers touch the heights. They destroyed Everton, turning on the kind of football in that game which was to carry them through Europe as the season progressed.

114

Charlie Cooke, the Chelsea ball artist who was one of the members of the Stamford Bridge European Cup Winning Cup team who told the Rangers' players that they could win the trophy.

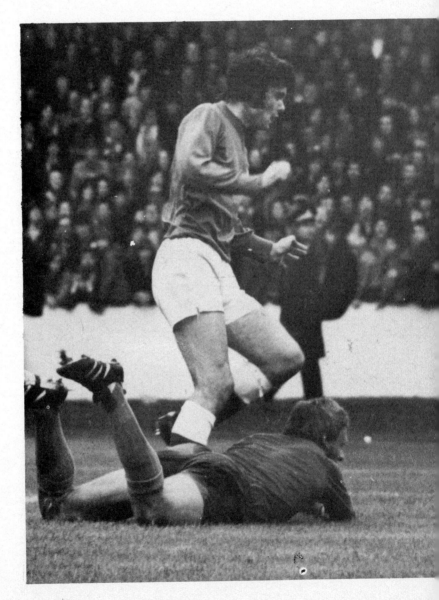

Rangers' centre-forward Derek Johnstone beats Everton's 'keeper Gordon West to score his side's first goal.

Everton fielded their full team and they had played two warm-up matches before travelling north. One had been against a select team in Dublin and the other a closed-doors' match against Blackburn Rovers. Neither helped them much as they wilted under the power that Rangers displayed that night.

For a team who had failed so often against English opposition Rangers really turned it on . . . and no one more so than young Derek Johnstone, still, at this early stage of the season, known only as a centre-forward.

Although he was facing the vastly experienced English international centre-half Brian Labone, the teenager scored both Rangers' goals, the first in thirty-nine minutes and the second in fifty-four minutes. Although Joe Royle scored for Everton when Rangers relaxed their grip on the game in the closing five minutes to make the final result 2–1, the score line did not give a proper picture of the total superiority that Rangers showed that night.

It was a magnificent performance and it was probably best summed up for me the next day at Tynecastle when I went to Edinburgh to see Spurs—next visitors to Ibrox—take on Hearts. After that game I was with Alan Gilzean, Spurs' Scottish international forward and 'Gilly' was desperate to hear more about how Rangers had played against the Goodison Park side.

He told me: 'Our boss (Manager Bill Nicholson) was there to see the game and he came back and told us that Rangers were so far ahead of Everton that they could have been five goals up at half time. He said that if they had taken all the chances in the game they would have won quite comfortably by half-a-dozen goals. We could hardly believe it . . .'

The Nicholson summing-up had clearly shaken Gilzean and his Spurs' team-mates. In previous clashes between the London club and the Ibrox side Spurs had had the edge even when the games were played in Glasgow. Now they felt they might be up against it. That game against Hearts was their opener and they lost 2–1 but vowed that they would take their revenge on Rangers . . . in spite of their manager's warning. It was as if the Rangers' display against Everton had made the Londoners determined to rise to the challenge and with their latest big money buy Ralph Coates from Burnley in the team they thought that they could do better than Everton.

Again, like Everton, they had out their best team with eight internationals in the line-up and such star names as Pat Jennings, Alan Mullery, Mike England, Martin Chivers, Martin Peters, Coates and Gilzean. Yet, even with that glittering line-up, Bill Nicholson, heedful of the Rangers' display against Everton elected to play a defensive game and look for a draw.

When any team does that in a pre-season challenge game, the type of game that normally calls for a side's attacking flair to be paraded in front of the fans, then it can only be taken as a tribute to the strength of the opposition.

Rangers, though, didn't sit back to accept compliments. They roared into attack against Spurs with the same enthusiasm and appetite they had shown against Everton. They were always on top of the game, always pushing into dangerous attacks and another fifty thousand fans were able to celebrate a victory double over the English when Willie Johnston scored in seventy-one minutes after little Tommy McLean had master minded the move. Again it was a single goal victory . . . but it was a good victory and one which came against a team which ended the season as winners of the European Union Cup.

So, with these two pre-season games Rangers' vast support was given a guide to how their team was to gain success in Europe in the later stages of the season.

Against Everton they saw for the first time the marvellous manner in which their team rose to the pinnacle of their form when faced with top level opposition. . . .

Against Spurs they saw how the current Ibrox team were able to overcome a packed defence, something that had been the scourge of Rangers' teams down the years.

Then later in the season there came a further guide for Europe from the English First Division. It came in the spell between the second round of the European Cup Winners Cup and the quarter finals. There is a long gap between these two rounds, a gap which stretches from November to March, one designed to aid those countries who have winter shut-downs in their season. Rangers' manager Willie Waddell wanted a top class fixture to fill that gap, and suddenly a tailor-made game was set up for him and his team!

As he put out feelers for a match which would help keep his team keyed up for the tough European clashes still to come the ideal opportunity arrived in an invitation from Chelsea for Rangers to play at Stamford Bridge. The game was to be a testimonial for Chelsea's long-serving skipper Ron Harris and with Chelsea being the holders of the European Cup Winners Cup it was a chance for Rangers to measure themselves

Alfie Conn shoots for goal as the Spurs defender comes in to tackle.

against the team who held the trophy they dreamed of winning.

Chelsea had been knocked out of the current tournament in the second round after one of the season's shock European results. They had been eliminated by Atavidaberg, an all-amateur team from Sweden on the away goals counting double rule. Now they wanted to show the whole of the Continent, as well as their own fans, that it was all a dreadful mistake. That, really, they should still be in the tournament and they intended to do so at the expense of Rangers, the sole remaining British team in the competition.

The previous season they had won the trophy in style in a replayed final against the fabled Spanish masters, Real Madrid. In the Athens' final they had been fortunate to draw 1–1 in the first game and then had won 2–1 in the replay. Most of the players who had won in Athens lined up in the side to face Rangers.

The Scots survived a disturbed afternoon at their London hotel when a bomb scare directed against the team found the players out on the street when they were supposed to be resting before the game.

They shrugged off that upset and in front of sixteen thousand fans at Stamford Bridge, including a massive following of their own supporters, they hurled into attack after attack. With Willie Henderson having his best game of the season to make it an unhappy testimonial for his direct opponent Harris, Rangers were always on top. Colin Stein hit the post with a header. Willie Johnston hit the same post with a shot and then Alex MacDonald saw Marvin Hinton clear a header, which had beaten Peter Bonetti, off the line.

These three escapes looked like robbing Rangers of the victory their play and their pressure had earned them. But suddenly as the game edged into injury time Sandy Jardine came upfield to force the ball over the line for the winner. That goal meant a hat-trick of victories over English First Division opposition for the Ibrox team . . . and it also spelled out once again the power they had available for these prestige games and for the glory games in Europe!

They had defeated the European Cup Winners Cup holders on their own ground and it was another of the signs that pointed, even that early, towards Barcelona and the victory that awaited them there. Certainly the Chelsea manager, Dave Sexton one of England's most respected thinkers on the game, had no doubts about Rangers' European prospects at the

Spurs goalkeeper punches the ball away from the head of Derek Johnstone (Rangers) during this raid on the Spurs goal.

champagne party which was thrown for the players after the game.

I spoke to Sexton and his experienced assistant Ron Suart at that reception and both tipped Rangers to take the trophy. Said Sexton: 'Right from the start of the tournament I have been watching Rangers' progress very carefully. Originally, of course, I was watching them because I reckoned that they would be one of the danger teams to any hopes I had of keeping the cup at the Bridge. That dream has gone for us now . . . but I still believe that Rangers will keep the Cup Winners Cup in Britain for the third year in succession. Manchester City won it and then we had it last season and now I think that it will prove to be Rangers' turn. They were very impressive against us tonight and I have looked very closely at

Alec Macdonald (Rangers) shoots at the Everton goal as Newton (No. 3 Everton) comes in to tackle.

Willie Johnston (Centre Rangers) is surrounded by two
Tottenham Hotspur players.

the last eight of the tournament. Torino and Bayern Munich will be the main threats to Rangers . . . but I don't think that they need be afraid of anyone if they play the way they played against us tonight.

'They deserved to beat us and, make no mistake, we wanted to win the game. We wanted to win it for Ronnie's sake because it was his testimonial match and we wanted to win it, as well, to show our supporters that we should still be in Europe. We didn't manage it.'

The Chelsea manager was not the only man at Stamford Bridge to tip a Rangers' victory. Scottish star Charlie Cooke, who had master minded that replay victory over Real Madrid just six months earlier, told the Rangers' players that he thought they were good enough to win. Most of his team-mates agreed. . . .

Rangers' boss Willie Waddell realised that, once more, he had seen his team boost the prestige of Rangers. It was a boost that reminded the fans in England that although Chelsea and Liverpool had been knocked out of the Cup Winners Cup, Britain still had a representative . . . and a team capable of winning the trophy. It was a boost, too, for the players as they had their minds brought back to Europe in spite of the long gap between the second round and the quarter finals.

But, most of all, it was a warning which echoed round Europe . . . a warning to the other teams left in the last eight of the tournament that Rangers were a force to be reckoned with. A look at their achievements at this stage was impressive in any language. No one could have doubts about this Rangers' team now. If they did then they could always talk to Dave Sexton. . . .